(Re)narrating Teacher Identity

SOCIAL JUSTICE
ACROSS CONTEXTS IN EDUCATION

sj Miller & Leslie David Burns
GENERAL EDITORS

Vol. 6

The Social Justice Across Contexts in Education series is
part of the Peter Lang Education list.
Every volume is peer reviewed and meets
the highest quality standards for content and production.

PETER LANG
New York • Bern • Frankfurt • Berlin
Brussels • Vienna • Oxford • Warsaw

(Re)narrating Teacher Identity

Telling Truths and Becoming Teachers

Edited by Audrey Lensmire and Anna Schick

Thank you
for all you do!
Audrey Lensmire

PETER LANG

New York • Bern • Frankfurt • Berlin
Brussels • Vienna • Oxford • Warsaw

Library of Congress Cataloging-in-Publication Data

Names: Lensmire, Audrey, editor. | Schick, Anna, editor.
Title: (Re)narrating teacher identity: telling truths and becoming teachers /
edited by Audrey Lensmire and Anna Schick.
Description: New York: Peter Lang, 2017.
Series: Social justice across contexts in education; vol. 6
ISSN 2372-6849 (print) | ISSN 2372-6857 (online)
Includes bibliographical references.
Identifiers: LCCN 2017003522 (print) | LCCN 2017017130 (ebook)
ISBN 978-1-4331-3499-9 (hardcover: alk. paper)
ISBN 978-1-4331-3498-2 (paperback: alk. paper) | ISBN 978-1-4331-4034-1 (ebook pdf)
ISBN 978-1-4331-4035-8 (epub) | ISBN 978-1-4331-4036-5 (mobi)
Subjects: K-12 teaching; Urban Teaching; Preservice Teacher Education; Teacher
Education Curriculum; Student teacher; Student teacher evaluation; Beginning Teacher;
Teaching Experience; Teacher Identity; Teacher Survival: Mental Health; Writing
pedagogy; Narrative writing; Writing Workshops
College teaching—Social aspects. | College teachers—Psychology. | Identity (Psychology)
Academic writing—Psychological aspects. | Discrimination in higher education.
Classification: LCC LB2331 .R465 2017 (print) | LCC LB2331 (ebook)
DDC 378.1/25019—dc23
LC record available at https://lccn.loc.gov/2017003522
DOI 10.3726/b10687

Bibliographic information published by **Die Deutsche Nationalbibliothek**.
Die Deutsche Nationalbibliothek lists this publication in the "Deutsche
Nationalbibliografie"; detailed bibliographic data are available
on the Internet at http://dnb.d-nb.de/.

The paper in this book meets the guidelines for permanence and durability
of the Committee on Production Guidelines for Book Longevity
of the Council of Library Resources.

Printed in the United States of America

For all the Wild Horses

Acknowledgments

Audrey: Tim for everything, Karen for starting The Group, Anna for inspiring the Wild Horses, sj, and ACE

Amanda: The Wild Horses, Jake, Mom, Dad, sisters Needle, and Wally

Anna: Ms. Scott, Christian, Audrey, Tim, The Wild Ones, and the regular and special "K's"

Aubrey: The Wild Horses, Michael, Mom, Dad, Betsy, and anyone who helped me see my way through the rough patch

Marie: The Wild Horses, Adam, Mom, Dad, Maggie, and families new and old

Sam: My dear family, Greta, Leo, Oscar, and my Wild Horses

Table of Contents

List of Tables and Figures

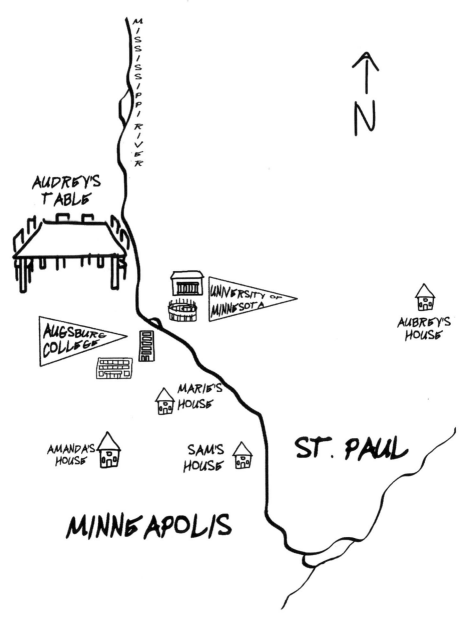

Figure 1: Map
Source: Jake Mohan

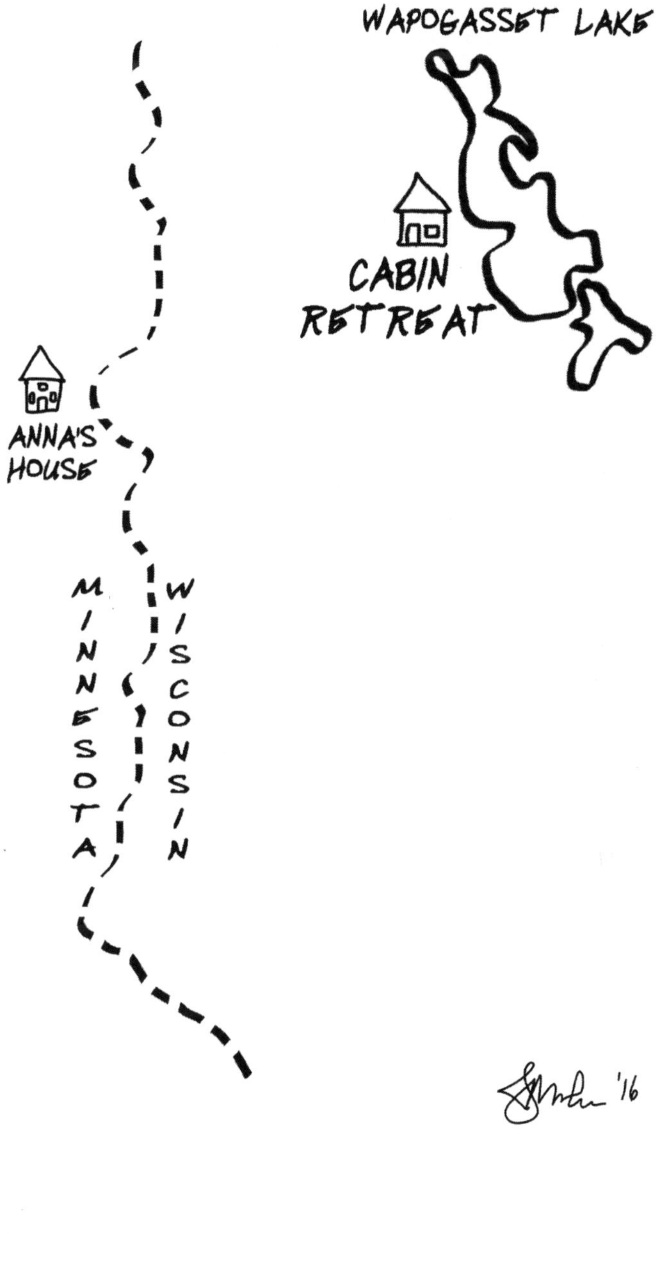
WAPOGASSET LAKE
CABIN RETREAT
ANNA'S HOUSE
MINNESOTA
WISCONSIN
'16

Foreword

BY ANGELA COFFEE, ERIN STUDELBERG,
AND COLLEEN CLEMENTS

In the tentative heat of late June, our group (Angela, Erin, and Colleen) paused just outside of the home of Anna and our introduction to the authors of this book. The bringing together of our collectives had been in the works for a long time. Our two groups had both been working to use stories and writing to help us make sense of the role of women in education. Through conversations with Audrey and her husband Tim (who was also our former professor), the three of us had been catching glimpses into the work of these women teachers for the past several years. Many of the group's questions, concerns, struggles, and hopes seemed to vibrantly connect with, overlap, and flow concurrently with our own. As we stood together at the base of the charming Victorian staircase that would lead us up to the group of women waiting inside, we lingered momentarily, anticipating the evening and conversations ahead, wondering at what might emerge.

Four years earlier, the three of us had found one another within a "Foundations of Education" course we had taken with Tim near the beginning of our doctoral programs at the University of Minnesota. Our shared interests and connections led us to develop independent studies, cultivate collectives, organize conference presentations, and create research projects together. Our experiences as a collective—a group deeply committed to one another and to challenging hetero-patriarchal white supremacy in education—radically transformed, illuminated, and nourished our journeys through graduate school. Collective memory work (Haug, 1987, 2008, n.d.), a feminist methodology for theorizing lived experiences and the ideologies entangled within them, has been foundational in our work together. In this process, individual written narratives of memory are collectively imagined, analyzed, and reimagined in an attempt to attune us to the dominant and normalizing narratives living within our stories and to create new possibilities for humanizing pedagogy. For us as white women teachers and researchers, this dependable community of care and deep accountability has been critical. Through this journey, our writing, our memories, our theoretical commitments, and our lives have been knit together in ways that blurred the edges of individual scholarship and enabled us to experience collective interdependence by sharing our stories with one another in deep trust, vulnerability, and desire for a better world.

As we stood at the foot of Anna's staircase, Audrey burst out onto the porch. "I just knew you were here!" she declared. With a huge smile, she ushered us into Anna's house. In the living room, we ate dinner and we talked. We sat in a circle and shared our stories with one another. Despite having never met before, there was a shared recognition and sense of support between our groups. We recognized in this collection of women the mutual care, generative and ongoing inquiry, and collective entanglement of stories that have characterized much of our work together. And we saw the power that collectivity has had for them as they have supported and challenged one another and reimagined their storied lives as women teachers.

In many ways the (re)narrated stories told in this book also resonate deeply with the three of us and connect to the work that we have done exploring our own lived experiences as white women teachers—a cohort historically constructed as caring nurturers of children, reproducers of patriarchy and white supremacy, and sources of cheap labor in the building of a colonial nation state. When we explore this narrative, we like to borrow Erica Meiner's (2002) use of the "White Lady Bountiful" teacher trope: she is a virtuous, kind, and feminine woman who holds the future of the nation (her students) in her hands, and through that power reproduces hegemony. This narrative positions the white woman teacher in a contradictory role in the classroom: she is expected to control her students while being controlled by her superiors; she is the purveyor of a hetero-patriarchal culture that also limits and oppresses her as a woman. We recognize that the White Lady Bountiful lives in each of us and we see how her narrative persists through the stories, memories, and artifacts of the beginning women teachers in this book. In addition to her history, today the white woman teacher has also been constructed as a "problem" in schools because there are too many of her and because she is limited in her understanding of race outside the normalizing power of her whiteness. The stories in this book contribute much to this important conversation about the white woman teacher, how she is positioned as a "problem," and the histories that live in and through her. Each chapter offers us a new understanding of how her construction also connects to another issue that many women and women teachers face: personal struggles with their mental and emotional health.

The multitude of emotions and experiences of being a teacher that the authors here explore in their (re)narrated stories include anger, sadness, despair, addiction, hopelessness, anxiety, depression, discomfort, joy, relief, success, and desire. These affective experiences can and ought to be understood alongside both historical and contemporary narratives of white women teachers. As teachers and teacher educators, we share these feelings and have supported our students as they have, too. In particular, these stories have illuminated an important source of tension in our understanding of mental health. Because Western patriarchal culture centers the individual as knower, thinker, and doer, the emotional and embodied experiences of teachers easily become individualized, too. The dominant conception of mental health is of an individual's journey, one that often holds us in a narrative of shame and self-blame rather than allowing us to disrupt, complicate, and expand our understanding of how and why we struggle. But like the historical, cultural, and political narratives of women teachers that live in and through us, our mental health can also be understood in more complex and collective ways. The stories in this book live in this tension between reproducing individual conceptions of mental health and seeking radical new possibilities for imagining self, including mental health, as a collective entanglement of systems, histories, and narratives.

Within this entanglement, we all embody multiple identities, both throughout our lives and from moment to moment as our daily contexts shift. This multiplicity of identities is present in any given moment. We are daughters, sisters, mothers, teachers, writers, and countless other labels we might give ourselves. When embodying the role of teacher, these other identities do not go away; yet, as articulated throughout this work, the socially constructed role of teacher seems to demand a suppression of the parts of us that do not easily comport with the White Lady Bountiful, the picture of the perfect maternal yet virginal presence, beneficently overseeing her charges, with infinite patience and caring, yet somehow able to remain neutral and detached, denying any expression of human emotion.

The chapters in this book are, in various ways, an attempt to interrupt the notion of a "perfect teacher" that suppresses all other identities. Persistent and dominant historical narratives, their influence strengthened by repetition and aimed at universalization, reproduce an (often problematic) unified identity: in this case, one that is either an attempt at embodying the role of "perfect teacher," or an embrace of the complete failure to do so. As teachers, and as humans, we fall somewhere in between the two, and neither of them are a true representation of our lived experience. Our identities as we embody them are always partial and becoming, rather than whole and fixed. And yet there is something about the act of "storying" our experience that seems to bend us toward these universalizing narratives, that silences not only the more complicated parts of our own stories as white teachers, but also the counter-narratives from more marginalized perspectives. We have found that the act of narrating stories always risks the reproduction of dominant narratives; even as we attempt to disrupt them, we can find our stories harnessed to narratives of oppression and violence. Perhaps retelling our stories collectively, as the authors have done here, offers a way to interrupt that reproduction.

So, as you read these stories, we would like to offer an invitation. Our practice of collective storytelling and reading invokes in us a desire for you, too, to "read collectively." This invitation to read collectively, even though you are likely reading this alone, encourages you to think about your own experience alongside the stories presented here, and your own multiple identities, attuned to the shifting spaces between and amidst your stories and the stories in this book. For it is in this act of reading and thinking collectively that we might better come to know the multitude of identities that reside in us all and the ways in which we perpetuate and resist universalizing stories—and in so doing, work to disrupt the power of the dominant narratives that continue to shape our storied existences.

Angela C. Coffee
Erin B. Stutelberg
Colleen D. Clements
August 2016

REFERENCES:

Haug, F. (2008). *Memory Work*. Australian Feminist Studies, *23*(58), 537–541.

Haug, F. (1987). *Female Sexualization: A Collective Work of Memory*. London: Verso.

Haug, F. (n.d.) *Memory-Work as a Method of Social Science Research: A detailed Rendering of Memory-Work Method*. Research guide.

Meiners, E. R. (2002). Disengaging from the legacy of lady bountiful in teacher education classrooms. *Gender and Education, 14*(1), 85–94.

In this powerful first of-its-kind collection in teacher education, new and experienced teachers reveal how their mental health and well-being intersected with learning to teach and teaching; and how they found each other along the way. Through their raw but carefully crafted stories, Aubrey, Anna, Audrey, Amanda, Marie and Samantha share their vulnerabilities with a sort of brazen honesty that invites us into their individual and collective truth-telling. So often vulnerability and honesty are damned and verboten in the professional lives of teachers.

They have shown us how writing, collaboration, and friendship provided them, over time, a strength that offset their fears and struggles in the classroom. In each other, they found safe harbor from many storms. In each other, they found mirrors filled with love and understanding. By witnessing each other, they (re) narrate what it means to be teacher.

Reading these narratives gives us all the freedom and permission to release the wild horses from within. I'm inspired to run with them. I know that I saw myself unfold in these pages and that they allowed me to feel more human, too.

To my newfound Wild Horses, thank you for demystifying stigma, opening honest dialogue, and showing us true humanity.

We are forever indebted to you.

sj Miller, Ph.D.
Social Justice Across Context in Education Series, Co-Editor

CHAPTER ONE

On Becoming a Group of Women

BY AUDREY LENSMIRE

I liked the feel of the horse's soft mouth as it grabbed apples or sugar cubes or carrots out of my hand. I liked the sounds of the horse breathing. I liked to see the twitching of its powerful muscles and the continuous flicking of its tail to push away flies. I consider myself a city child, but I love horses. I was lucky to have lessons at Harms Woods, a stable outside of Chicago, situated at a busy suburban intersection but connected to a forest preserve. I loved cleaning out the horseshoes and brushing down the animal after a lesson. I liked memorizing the names of the parts of the bridle and saddle. I had a crop and wore dusty jeans and a helmet when I rode. My dad's parents, who I called Mutton and Poppy, praised me for my riding. It reminded them of when they were young and rode horses along Lake Michigan on vacation in Door County, Wisconsin. Once, when they came to watch my lesson, Mutton, the never-afraid-outspoken-tough-Chicago woman, insisted to the teacher that I be given a show horse, not one of the lethargic trail horses I had been riding. I loved the height and pounding surefootedness of that horse. I was sure that I could go places on that one. But after too short a while my mom said we couldn't afford the Saturday lessons anymore. I think she was afraid of me learning to jump.

~~~

My story of how the six of us came together to write a book about becoming and being teachers begins years ago. The purpose of this chapter is to explain how our group came to be and who we are as a collective. As I tell our story, I will interrupt it and punctuate it with other stories that flow beneath, stories that began as mine and that allowed me to feel deeply connected to these women. This, and each of the chapters ahead, holds stories that ought to be considered honest, raw, real stories of our lives as teachers. We are very human teachers. We emphasize "human" to mark ourselves as simultaneously flawed and good enough. We feel connected by our hopes to teach well and by the continual struggles that shape our individual and collective experiences. And it is my hope that the insights of Anna, Amanda, Marie, Aubrey, and Samantha, whose stories make up the bulk of this book, circle back to and inform how we in teacher education interact with and think about our students.

Our book aims to tell stories and recreate some of the feel of our group for you, so perhaps you might feel less alone.

~~~

Tim and I were driving east toward his hometown in rural Wisconsin, where we had agreed to do professional development work with teachers in its public elementary school. Tim wanted to talk. I thought we were going to review and rehearse the plans we had created for the two-day workshop. Instead, he asked me about my next writing and research project. I had recently started my second year as a professor in the education department at a small private college in Minneapolis. During my first year there, my dissertation had been published as a book and my mom had died from ovarian cancer. It had been hard to think about what was next.

I had been playing around with an idea to examine my teaching journals. I thought a look backward would help me better understand my new position as an educator of teachers. Even though I wanted to be a professor for years, I felt unsure. I couldn't remember the concerns I had as a teacher education student and novice teacher. I had gone as far as gathering up my journals and lesson plan books, organizing them by year and by school, and paging through entries (so many of which began with "I'm so tired"). But after an initial flurry of excitement, the project felt impossible and lonely and self-absorbed. I knew that I could not sustain a serious self-study of my years teaching elementary school.

"I am most interested in the young women in front of me, my students." This statement popped out of my mouth, surprising us both.

~~~

There had been a steady stream of young white women in and out of my office. Sometimes they were in tears. Some seemed to trust me and told me about their lives. I heard how they were dealing with the stress of assignments and readings. I listened as they asked me questions about how to become good teachers. For others, the frustrations were with how teacher education seemed disconnected from their notions of justice and their vision of being with young people in schools. Still others weren't coping well with the combined demands of courses, classroom observations and service, and local urban elementary schools that seemed chaotic and sometimes inane. Inhumane.

I figured that the way my classes were set up had signaled to these students that I might be a person they could talk to, someone who might lend an empathetic ear. In the elementary literacy education courses I taught we sat in a circle. Modeling my college teaching after a nontraditional, democratic workshop pedagogy, my classes usually opened with a meeting ("Anyone have an issue to raise, questions, or announcements to share?") in an effort to build community. Students participated in individual and group work, talking and writing to wrestle with problems and questions of practice.

I wondered about these women in our professional program, the ones who wanted to talk with me. They had already completed a bachelor's degree, were in and out of more or less unsatisfying jobs, and had decided to work toward a license to teach and then possibly finish a master's degree. I had followed a similar path two decades before. Who were they? Why were they here? What did they need and want to learn?

~~~

Karen had asked to speak to me after class. She was sitting across from me, but close, as my office is quite small. Her back was against my bookshelf (I noticed the spine of bell hooks' *Teaching to Transgress* behind her left shoulder), and she was talking, animatedly, about how frustrated she was about the lack of discussion of social justice in her classes, how excited she was to become a teacher, how she tried to make connections between course readings and her work in schools, and how she wanted her lesson plans to capture all of her thinking. I noticed she was passionate about lesson planning. She would go home at night wanting to talk it all through, but her boyfriend just didn't seem interested or willing to listen to her and how important all of this was. I was moved by her energy, her rapid talk, by her hands moving all around, and by her blue eyes looking at me, pleading with me.

She seemed like me and not like me. I was at least twenty years older than her and I had already been trying to figure out what was going on with these young women in front of me, who reminded me of me—full of fret and volume and a burgeoning sense of the world, the world of schools and teachers and children. She was so upset about how messed up it was, and I had been like that too (and I still am, although that upset is now expressed as anger and lived out with hard work to change things, little by little). But there she was saying that her boyfriend didn't seem to hear her. And I wanted to respond—because she was in one of my classes, because she was like me and not like me, because I felt responsible, and because

I was able to respond. I said, "Karen, what do you think about forming a group, outside of classes, where we talk about becoming teachers? I mean, I could help organize something. We could meet at my house. I have this big dining room table."

~~~

It's silly but when Tim and I got together, the life I imagined for us as intellectuals seemed pulled directly from an old movie, complete with the basement office lit by a single hanging bulb. We smoked and wore pencils behind our ears. In the shadows, an underling ran the mimeograph machine, rolling out fliers with blue ink to announce the next protest. At the time, I didn't know the living activists and organizers I do now, but at the core of my daydreams was what I wanted to do and how I wanted to live—to talk, to teach, to write, to protest.

I decided there was only one *thing* I really cared about when Tim and I moved into our house together: that we have a big dining room table. Around it, we—writers, academics, students, poets, activists, and friends—would gather to share meals, to tell stories, to change the world.

~~~

Karen said yes. We immediately went to work by writing a short list of women she and I knew (or knew of) in the program who we thought might be interested in talking and writing with other future teachers. There wasn't a long conversation about who to include or not include. A list of eight or so female graduate students was quickly generated. I had told Karen that we could talk and write about our experiences—and we'd "talk smart" and that it was okay to talk smart, as I was coming to understand myself. We could talk, theorize, and make sense of our/their experiences. Soon afterward, in January 2013, I sent out this email to the women on our list:

> I'm writing to you today to invite you to join a future-women-teachers' writing group. This whole thing started when I realized I've met so many amazing, intelligent, intense, and passionate women through my teaching at Augsburg. These women seem to have two things in common—their desire to be a teacher and their intense questioning of the world around them. I also sensed a desire for more connection, perhaps outside of the confines of a classroom and "official" work, for collective dialogue and companionship.

This message told the truth about Karen's and my goals for the group, but much more was bubbling for me beneath the surface. I felt troubled when Karen reported that her boyfriend did not seem to hear her. I immediately had ideas about how to change my teaching when Karen talked to me about "the lesson plan." I was curious and worried about the official and unofficial roles I would take on with the women in (what unceremoniously became known as) *The* Group. Was I their professor, a convener, a researcher, maybe (I hoped) a friend? And I was angry about teacher education, as a field and how we were living it out in our college, as the state attempted to standardize and routinize our work together.

I have thought a lot about how Karen said her boyfriend did not seem to hear her. The frustration that Karen expressed about her boyfriend hit close to home. In my first marriage and other significant relationships, I had experienced the feeling of not being listened to, of feeling silenced and becoming voiceless. I had come to believe that when I narrated my days with children and tried to figure things out about teaching, students, and lesson planning, I made myself undesirable, too much, too repetitive, too intense. This sadness about my retro-loneliness shot out of my heart and into the space between Karen and me, and then, like an other-mother, sister, friend, I wanted to say—he better listen to you with deep interest and love and admiration or he's not right for you. (It turned out that Karen was much smarter than I was—she left him soon after without any such intervention on my part.)

Karen's passion for talk about lesson plans suggested that I had misunderstood something in my teaching. I dreaded teaching lesson planning. It had always seemed like a rote, point-accumulating, technical activity. But Karen caused me to rethink my perspective. Lesson plans can carry meanings that are powerful and creative and are the weaving together of theories, the children in front of us, and past practices. Lesson plans can contain a voice of hope. Teachers can write lesson plans that say: through this plan and the messy improvisations required to pull any of it off, I hope that children will learn and grow and find meaning from being in school and being in the world.

In my classes, I began to say that the lesson plan is the main genre of our field. I embraced the idea that teaching future teachers how to write a lesson plan had power and potential for them to become agents of change. We would no longer go through the motions: "Here is where you write *the standard*. The *objective* goes there. Use a verb." Instead: "Here is a template and each heading contains history, a struggle for power, and multiple meanings." I encouraged students to consider how each copy/paste, each "just get this done," each refusal to consider alternatives was to remain passive and controlled. To copy and paste a standard was to consent to carrying out the legislative orders of the state. To copy and paste an objective from a textbook was to carry out decisions made by people far, far away. To assess a child's ability to make certain word families correctly was to consent to a white-supremacist, scientific-behaviorist assertion that all children learn to read best in a certain (white) way as long as you keep going over those pesky phonemes.

~~~

The first meeting of The Group was January 24, 2013 at the dining room table. Just three young women and me. Over the course of the next two years, we held monthly meetings. During that beginning time The Group consisted of Karen,

Marie, Amanda, Aubrey, Samantha, and Kate (Karen and Kate chose not to participate in this book project, but their voices resonated deeply for me across these first two years). I had applied to the college's institutional research board (IRB) so I could take notes and record the meetings. As a professor in a tenure-track position, I was required to conduct research, present "findings" at professional conferences, and write to publish the results of the research. I understood that I had to keep careful track of what happened in the meetings and where they led. I was excited to learn from and alongside the women in The Group.

My initial request to research what happened with The Group was sent back from the IRB committee for clarification: the committee, at first, didn't know how to make sense of the open-ended, hypothesis-less nature of my research proposal. I described how I was going to function as a member of the group, a leader, a researcher, and a participant. I did not know what I would find. Eventually, my project was approved and I set out to be a "good" ethnographer by taking field notes, writing research memos, sifting through data for generative themes as I had learned in graduate school. But the truth was that researching the group was not an orderly process. I was invested, enthralled, overwhelmed, busy, tired, and completely given over to it. It's not that my role as researcher went away. I could call myself a "participant observer" as many ethnographers do, but even that title still seemed to distance me from all of this. I decided to keep recording, taking notes, and keep going with the women until they wanted to stop.

Some of my own thinking, writing, and presenting about The Group diverges from the purpose of this book. I've started to explore more carefully the place of mental health and mental illness (as I share a bit later) in my life and the lives of these women. But I liked the *blurring* (thanks Shannon McManimon), the *dissolving* (thanks Angela Coffee) of these traditional subject/object, researcher/researched roles. I'm in this Group. I'm of this Group.

During the first six months of our meetings, from January through June 2013, we began to get to know each other. Because the women wanted to write, and I was used to teaching writing, we began each meeting with a writing exercise. We'd move from a writing prompt to talking. We did check-ins. For each of these early meetings, a slightly different and overlapping set of women showed up. I was surprised when I went back through my notes to see that Samantha and Aubrey didn't attend the same meeting, together, until April. So introductory rituals—writing, sharing, and checking in, were important to establishing our connections and in some ways still shape what happens when we meet.

In our third meeting, each woman shared why they were showing up at the table. Karen said she wanted "a space to talk about our profession around women" and Aubrey shared "I was missing intellectual things." Amanda wanted "a sense of community because I like being part of discussions in class." Samantha thought a group might be a good place for "networking and a support system."

Our early conversations wove in and out of coursework, frustrating assignments (How many times do I have to write my philosophy of education?), student-teaching stresses and joys, the edTPA, and the challenge of accepting feedback (which often felt like stinging personal criticisms). And then, surprisingly, we were soon talking about personal struggles with anxiety and depression in our lives and those of our loved ones; drug addiction and recovery; lovers and dreams for love; our working and middle-class, urban, suburban, and rural white racial identities; the layers and layers of complex issues arising among children, teachers, and families. (I beamed with joy when my daughters slipped in and out of the dining room, during our meetings, sometimes stealing snacks, listening in, saying a shy hello, witnessing a riot of women talking loud, laughing, swearing, crying, and writing.)

When the women began to disclose, around the edges, "I went on medication" or "I came to Minnesota to go to treatment" or "I am so anxious," I couldn't understand how this casually pulled together group of women could be so similar. We all had experienced anxiety and/or depression and, except for one of us, had been or were on medication to alleviate the at-times debilitating symptoms of these "dis-eases."

~~~

Much of what we talked about in those first few months was thrilling in the sense that I knew I had been right, instinctively, experientially, intuitively, to invite these women into my house and into my life. In bed, at night, after the young women drove off and my daughters were asleep, I would sometimes whisper to Tim that, my goodness, I was overwhelmed by their big lives, big emotions, their big worries about the present and the future. I would cry a little and tell him about how this new work was tapping into something very deep for me. I didn't want it to be true: I didn't wish that these young women shared these experiences with me. I realized that I had constructed a story of my life that said mental illness was unique to my family. My experiences with anxiety and depression, my ongoing "I can't get out of bed I'm too dizzy" panic attacks, were just me, were just a story that happened in a family like mine with a dad like mine, an uncle like mine, a sister like mine, a grandma, and a great-grandma like mine. I had distanced myself from my family—I wasn't really like them, because I was not manic-depressive, schizophrenic, bi-polar, crazy, institutionalized. But they were my family and I was them.

How could it be that all these beautiful and unique young women shared this thing with my family, with me? I have lived ashamed and in hiding about my dad and have tried to come to terms with what it meant to love him and to be afraid of him. It was confusing to hear my mom explain to me, "He was sick, he didn't take care of himself and I couldn't take care of three children." She called him a child, including him with my sister and me in a list of those she had to care for. So he was childlike and sick. She had been encouraged by not only her own parents, but by his, my Mutton and Poppy, to leave him. So she did. As a child, I was afraid that I might become "sick" like him. But I was also drawn to him, loyal to him, protective of him—he was tall and handsome, well-educated, a big talker about life and feelings.

My heart had already opened up to the women and I was, with Tim's help, just getting out from underneath these confusing, painful stories I had been making up and retelling myself since I was seven. The story I lived by was that my dad got sick because he worked too hard. He was very intelligent and he pushed himself too hard so he got sick. He was sick and couldn't work. He was unlovable to my mother. (He relied upon his parents a lot, where there was smoke and gin and yelling, so maybe they made him sick?) I would not push myself too hard.

I knew that we were the Prozac Nation—people were taking pharmaceuticals all the time but I really hadn't connected the dots until then. The young white women who were becoming teachers, the women in my classes, indeed, the women in front of me were like lots and lots of women in the United States today. They are anxious and depressed. They may or may not have the same long histories of mental illness as my family's, but they were suffering too. I suppose all of this is to say that I was initially scared to open up about my personal histories to the women in The Group. I've been on medication, straight, without a day's break since at least 2002. I've considered reducing or stopping but I don't. I like how I feel. When this medication kicked in, it felt like gauze or a cloud lifted from my mind. I felt clear. I felt like me.

What was I supposed to do? I had been their teacher and was now the convener, the participant, the researcher. And I was responsible to them and I had to figure out what that meant. I had to be honest with them. If I was going to continue to learn and teach, it meant telling truths.

~~~

As The Group continued to meet monthly, the women moved from being students to being student teachers. Then they were hired as long-call subs, behavior specialists, or semipermanent replacements in classrooms who had lost licensed teachers. It was a very bumpy road, throughout it we met, I took notes, and the new teachers tried to hold on and not burn out (already).

I had begun to make some connections between our personal struggles and the realities of our profession. I read about how our society and our profession have historically disciplined women. I explored the etymology of "crazy." I read popular and historical accounts of women's mental health. I went back to Madeleine Grumet (1998), who researched and wrote about early teacher education in *Bitter Milk: Women and Teaching*. She shared how the teaching journals of Cyrus Pierce, written during the common school movement in the 1830s, contained crucial clues as to why our profession has been treating our mostly female workforce the way it has for more than 150 years. Pierce confessed in his journals that teaching children was "exasperating, frustrating, and fatiguing." However, when he became a teacher of teachers (our first teacher educator) he developed a requisite list of teacher attributes. Grumet wrote:

> He lists the desirable qualities of teachers as health, good standing in the community, a well balanced mind "free from eccentricities and the infirmities of genius," deep interest in children, patience, mildness, firmness and perfect self-control. (p. 51)

During this time of study, I had also been talking seriously with Sarah, Tim's college-aged daughter, about feminism. Sarah was a double major in English and Gender and Women's Studies at the University of Wisconsin–Madison and she had been taking a series of exciting classes that we would talk about for hours. I realized how lacking my own scholarly engagement with feminism had been, so Sarah gave me her Women's Studies (WOST 101) Reader. Among the articles and essays in it, I responded most strongly to Charlotte Perkins Gilman's famous 1892 short story called "The Yellow Wall-Paper," which traced a woman's forced "rest" by her physician husband in an airy attic of a rented countryside estate. The character's experience—of feeling surrounded, of being alone and watched, of talking to herself as her sense of reality crumbled—resonated strongly with me. I realized that I might start drawing on what I already knew about white supremacy and institutional racism in order to better understand how patriarchy worked in our society. I began to connect all of my reading and conversations to what was going on with the women in The Group.

In my first book, I had taken up the complexities of being a white teacher working with students of color in city classrooms. I had carefully examined race, structural racism, and white lives. After reading Gilman's haunting story, I began exploring and making explicit to myself the ways that patriarchy and white supremacy were often similar—confining, unrelenting, sometimes invisible, at times inexplicable.

But I decided not to wait until I had everything figured out.

I shared a feminist critique of the school system and teacher education with The Group. I began to respond to some of the women's stories and struggles to learn to teach with phrases like: "Maybe you are not wrong—maybe you are right—maybe patriarchy is at play." Or I would prod, not wanting them to feel defeated again: "Maybe you feel insecure, anxious, depressed because of the stressful situations you are in—not because of something in you—maybe there is nothing wrong with you."

~~~

Then something happened to Aubrey that clarified everything about my role as a teacher educator and my worries about the education of teachers. One night Aubrey called me at home crying and I couldn't get her to stop. She was worried that she had failed student teaching. She had an observation earlier that day and she received an email that stated she had to report to the college on Friday for a meeting with the director of student teaching, her college student-teaching supervisor, and her advisor, due to her "lack of professionalism" and "emotional instability."

Aubrey told me that she had not felt ready for the day's observation. She was nervous. The classroom teacher had told her over and over to "go by the book" because new teachers can't make it if they don't just go by the book. Meanwhile, her supervisor was asking her how she was changing the lessons in the book to differentiate instruction for the range of children in the room.

During the observation, Aubrey knew it didn't go well. When she returned to the classroom after taking her children to the busses at the end of the day, she saw her classroom teacher and college supervisor talking—talking about her. She panicked. They told her that she needed to be more confident (something I still laugh out loud at, both on behalf of Aubrey but also because it is so absurd—to observe and evaluate someone, whose future you hold in your hands, and you tell them to be confident).

At this point in the semester, Aubrey, who didn't quite qualify for food stamps, was just getting by. She was eating the children's leftover snacks. She started to cry in this meeting with the classroom teacher and college supervisor. And then she got mad and vented. She said it was wrong to have novice teachers like her working with children who needed the best teachers, that these children depended on school more than children who come from upper- or even middle-class backgrounds, and here she was learning on their backs and failing them. She was mad at the system, mad at the district, and mad at the teacher education program that put her there, and she said something like "It's so fucked up."

Aubrey was enmeshed in Pierce's bullshit storyline about calm, eternally patient, smiling teachers. She was pissed that the children who needed the best teachers were the learning ground for a novice like her. She wasn't calm. She wasn't properly disciplined. Her use of language wasn't appropriate. She had been flooded with feedback, advice, criticism, theories, strategies, guidelines, rules, best practices, folk stories, not to mention her own negative self-talk, all of which spun around and in and clouded her ability to be present and creative and teach young children. It froze her up. Aubrey was barely getting by. Her future career and ability to get paid and eat were in question. But my colleagues, teacher-educators, wanted to discipline Aubrey in the name of Pierce, as if she could be threatened into finding within herself that "deep well of patience, obedience, self-abnegation and loving kindness."

I didn't and don't pretend to be any kind of therapist with the women, but over time I did more than just kindly empathize with their struggles. After that happened to Aubrey, I stopped being polite. At my college, I confronted my colleagues. I found my voice. In The Group I narrated and (re)narrated my stories of teaching, my stories of struggle. I stopped worrying about being what I thought was pedagogical. I started telling the truths. And I tried over and over to ask them to consider other reasons for their feelings of inadequacy. It turned out that truths are pedagogical.

~~~

Initially, Marie signed a contract to replace a teacher going on maternity leave. She was to shadow the teacher in her final week, but when she showed up on a Monday, the children hadn't been told their teacher would be leaving them with a new teacher in a few days. Marie was not introduced and the teacher went to a mid-day doctor appointment and didn't return. So Marie was the teacher the next day. There was so much chaos. Marie couldn't stop crying and called her mother who was also a teacher. Marie wrote the principal and told her that she wouldn't be coming back the next day. It was the hardest thing for Marie to do.

Samantha, Aubrey, and Amanda have similar stories of rocky transitions from student teacher to teacher. Aubrey got a part-time job teaching four-year olds as an arts and science specialty teacher (think art-on-a-cart). Amanda moved into a fifth-grade position in a school where she had volunteered as a Reading Corps member and then been employed as an educational assistant and testing coordinator. She helped Samantha get a middle-school special-education classroom in the same school. None of these first teaching positions lasted long. But you will read those stories soon. I am almost done with the story of our Group.

We had been meeting for two years and the women felt that they wanted to do something new. They wanted to do more with writing. It was just our luck that Anna came into our lives.

~~~

"I am most interested in the young women in front of me, my students." This statement popped out of my mouth, surprising both Tim and me.

As we talked and he drove along, I gazed out at the rolling hills, tree-topped ridges, and pastoral farmland of Wisconsin. I was looking forward to the horseback riding lessons his mom had set up for me. I figured that if we were going to be going back and forth for the length of this professional development work, then I would get back into riding. I thought of my mom then too; how she loved me and was afraid for me; how she didn't understand what it would have meant to me to jump.

~~~

The women have started to tease me. I take this as a good sign, a sign of closeness and love, of old boundaries blurring. They laugh at me and tell me that I am an "active listener" (they use air quotes when they say this), what with all my nodding and smiling and audible sighs and shouts of "Yes!"

~~~

The Group was ecstatic that Anna wanted to conduct a summer writing workshop for us. She had been a graduate student enrolled in Tim's Teaching Writing in Schools class. One night she shared in class that she was a former English teacher, and she wanted to learn more about gender, writing, and mental health. At the break, Tim walked over to Anna and said, "You really ought to talk with my wife Audrey. She's got this group…"

We wrote with Anna. Her teaching inspired our wild collective truth-telling about becoming and being teachers. That truth-telling follows.

Jump with us.

REFERENCES:

Grumet, M. (1998). *Bitter Milk: Women and Teaching*. Amherst, MA: University of Massachusetts Press.

Gilman, C. P. (2014). *"The Yellow Wallpaper" and Other Stories*. Mineola, NY: Dover Publications.

CHAPTER TWO

(Re)narration

BY ANNA SCHICK

Hello Audrey,

My name is Anna. I am currently in the Youth Development Leadership M.Ed. program at the University of Minnesota. Last night in Tim's Writing in Schools course, we shared possible topics for book group projects. I mentioned my interest in mental health/illness and how it is portrayed (or not portrayed) in non-fiction or fictional texts. Tim shared a brief summary of your work with women teachers. I am wondering if you would be willing to meet, I would love to hear more about what you are researching.

Would you be available Monday, February 16 to discuss? I am free daytime and happy to come to your office. Let me know if this works for you.

Looking forward!

Best regards,

Anna

BEGINNINGS

I typed this email in the write, delete, rewrite, delete fashion. Audrey's work, and frankly Audrey herself, intrigued me. A professor who was inviting and listening in on storylines about becoming a teacher in her dining room? I sent the email off the morning following Tim's Writing in Schools course. In class, we, teachers playing the evening role of students, had shared our writing interests in an effort to plan an upcoming book group. Ultimately, our group landed on Jeff Park's *Writing at the Edge*, a brave text that explores the experiences and writing of members of the Writer's Group associated with the Canadian Mental Health Association.

Speaking up in class on that February winter evening drew me not only to book group but to a new teacher group—a wild, honest collective with an abundance of stories to tell.

~~~

I arrived early for our meeting. I parked in a campus lot and checked the cars next to me for stickers. It was contract-only parking but I didn't anticipate to be long. I pulled my hood over my head and braved the brisk air. The morning sun was peeking through the garden-level windows of Audrey's office. She offered me a seat at a small round table. I sat and stared past her to the wall of book spines. I don't remember who spoke first, but we dropped our guards quickly and soon we were carrying on like old friends—the kind of talk where the coffee goes cold. She told me about the group of pre-service teachers who had been convening for two years at her dining room table. She shared anecdotes of the evening conversations as she wrote their names on her notepad. I shared my abbreviated history—I had been a teacher for eight years; I was a graduate student at the University of Minnesota; I was married to a German and had recently moved back from Switzerland; I tried to be a writer in the crevices of the day.

We took messy notes and reached across the little table to write on each other's yellow notepads. At one point, I copied down a diagram Audrey sketched. It was a Venn diagram but with three overlapping circles—one said "systems," another "medication," and the last "white female teacher." She explained that all the women in the group had disclosed experiences with mental illness from anxiety to depression. I listened and nodded, feeling at home in her stories of these women. In the margins I wrote questions like, "Why do women bury their mental health?"; "How do systems prepare teachers?"; and "How [underlined multiple times] can we write about this?" On the lower left-hand corner of the page, I was doing math—I had to design a 180-hour field experience for my graduate program. I wanted to lead a writer's workshop. The teachers wanted to write.

~~~

Hi Anna,

I hope you are well.

I met with the women's group last night. They definitely want to meet you and most are really excited to write (some nerves too).

We wonder if you can you come to our next meeting? It is Tuesday, March 2 from 7–9 p.m. at my house.

Let us know!
Thanks,
Audrey

I was quite nervous about meeting the group of women. I'd like to think of myself as a confident, prepared teacher but in this context I was seeking to be genuine, authentic, vulnerable. On the way there, I practiced introducing myself out loud in my car. "I've been a teacher for eight years. I've also struggled with my mental health." Do I tell them I was hospitalized? Twice? Or that I returned to graduate school to get away from teaching for a while?

We sat at Audrey's dining room table, a sturdy wooden table soaked with stories. I spoke first. The introduction sounded nothing like I had practiced in the car. I spilled too much—I remember telling a story about attending a funeral in college. He had committed suicide; it was the first time I saw the heartache I would have left behind if I had been successful. Too much. Definitely too much.

The table was full of teachers. Sam sat to my right, drawing intricate patterns up and down the side of her notebook. Karen was on a laptop, joining us from Salt Lake City. Marie, Amanda, Kate, and Aubrey sat across from me. Audrey sat to my left nodding and providing reassuring smiles for me to keep going. I transitioned from my confession of mental illness to my teaching career. I first described how I'd never wanted to share in a school setting that I was bipolar—always fearful that my big ideas would be interpreted as mania and my down days would invite suspicion of impending depression. I told them that I started teaching middle school language arts in St. Paul, Minnesota. I didn't go into the details of my first years of teaching, but I could have said something like: I wrote morning messages, developed an ulcer, broke up fights, built up community. Then, I moved to Switzerland and taught in an International School. I let them create the ooh-ah effect that comes with this statement, debating whether I should burst the bubble and reveal that teaching is teaching everywhere. I wanted them to know that I loved teaching but I, like so many teachers, was burnt, perhaps disenchanted.

As I listened to their introductions, Sam kept her head down and doodled. From a laptop screen, Karen told us about her newest invention to try to get know her third graders: Walk Home Wednesdays. She would draw a student's name from a bundle of popsicle sticks and then walk home with that student. She loved doing this, even though it cut into her prep time. But she still thought it was important and sighed, "We'll see how long I can keep it up." Marie expressed her discontentment with the contrast between what she was learning about the Montessori model in graduate school and what was actually happening in her classroom. Amanda worked on her laptop, preparing a fifth-grade history lesson plan for the next day throughout the entire conversation—doing her best to be a good teacher while remaining present. Aubrey talked about a student who ran in and out of her classroom, jumped on the tables, and threw scissors—she had ideas but was not the lead teacher. She wondered if she would spend all her days disciplining four-year olds. Audrey was teaching lesson planning to future teachers; she had a stack to grade and asked us about ways to give feedback. They were on a slow burn too, but not giving up or giving in.

~~~

As a young girl, I coached my sisters in the basement bedroom-turned-classroom on how to keep their pencils on the page when going for the loop on the *p* or the *b* or the tricky capital *R*. I mimicked the worksheets I received in school and wrote up questions about stories followed by long crooked lines for them to write the answer. After our summer-school sessions, I would head upstairs to my bedroom, balance my embroidered journal on the slant of my tanned thighs, and write my ten-year-old worries on the golden lines. Writing and teaching writing lived in very separate camps for me; in fact, they didn't even drink the same water. My loops on the page, as writer, were about life—how it wasn't fair that the boys got the outdoor pool for the swimming lessons and girls sweated in their one-piece suits inside. The writing was drawn from the well of experience. My sisters, as my students, wrote to reproduce knowledge. The words were drawn out of my old textbooks or from page 78 in the novel, where the answer was buried in the middle of the second paragraph. I even had a grade book where I would record the results of their writing. If a fight ever occurred outside of the imaginary school, I threatened to give them an "F" on their writing. This usually sent them into begging, "Nooo, not an F! We're sorry, we're sorry!" I reproduced the power I observed in my teachers, a power gained from assessing the rightness of writing.

~~~

Years later, I went to school to learn to become a *real* teacher. I learned about lesson plans and modification. I wrote papers that received extensive praise and felt I was on my way. My first practicum was observing an eighth-grade language arts teacher. She hung 100% reading quizzes on the door. She was teaching *The Giver* by Lois Lowry and sucking the life out of it. I started grading the teachers I observed, rating their performance of *teacher*. During my fall semester of my senior year of college, I started student teaching. This was the real deal: I would plan lessons and teach! I wanted to find the right clothes to wear, desperately wanting to play the part. Here's a story I wrote during the writer's workshop about my pre-service days:

> I was 21, a student teacher at a large high school in Madison, Wisconsin. Clad in my carefully-chosen-the-night-before long white skirt and mint-green bow-necked shirt, I slouched over a desk in the English department lounge. My head rested on my extended left arm, heavy with the day's exhaustion. The right hand held a red pen poised, ready to circle the misspellings and sentence fragments in the next victim's film analysis of *The Godfather*. The jagged-edged notebook pages slowly accumulated like snow across the desk; I was too tired to shovel them neatly into a stack. I spent every afternoon that week hovering over that little desk becoming a teacher.

The next week I sat upright in a padded armchair, ready for a meeting with my practicum supervisor and the head of the English Education Department. The meeting had been called to discuss my "professionalism." A teacher from the high school where I did my student teaching had notified my supervisor with a complaint: my tattoo had been seen on multiple occasions in the staff lounge. At the end of a deep exhale, my supervisor reminded me professional dress is important for teaching.

"But I am," I sputtered, "I am dressing professionally."

The head of the English Education Department took the opportunity to teach me, her student, "Well, clearly not if your tattoo is visible."

"What's wrong with having a tattoo?"

My defensive response signaled my tears to start welling.

"Now don't get emotional, it's just a matter of changing how you dress."

I choked, "What's wrong with getting emotional?"

"Nothing, I'm just saying you need to think about how you're presenting yourself."

A tributary made its way down my left cheek, and soon both sides were hot with fresh tears.

"But I'm working really hard, all the students even know what a flashback is."

Tattoos and tears are not *teacher*. Professional dress and keeping it together are teacher. As a pre-service teacher, my inner beliefs about the visibility of emotion and humanity in a teacher were regularly challenged. My cooperating teachers the following year gave me the first of many alternatives views on the embodiment of teacher.

~~~

When I became that first-year teacher, I was a seventh-grade middle-school language arts teacher. My ideas for writing ballooned, yet were quickly deflated when the results had to be squeezed into little rubric boxes. In one particular endeavor, I applied for a grant from a local literacy center. My student writers were contributors to a project titled *Old Stories/New Stories*, a body of refugee, immigrant, and relocation stories. I teetered in and around standards by calling the writing products *artifacts* instead of prescriptive genres. Yet even in my attempt to slightly bend the rules, I was still too often filling out the form of the teacher I had played as child with my sisters—the one in control, toting around a gradebook. It didn't *feel* right. I felt that writing was suffocated and fenced in, advising and counseling was on the fringe, and when critical conversation finally got going in our morning meeting the time was up and we had to move the desks and chairs back for the "real learning."

~~~

At age 25, I followed love to Switzerland. After completing a long-term sub position in first grade, I was hired on as a full-time teacher at an International School. I spent most of the time as the Literature A: English teacher for grades 11 and 12.

The critical views my international students brought to conversations on world literature repositioned my views on narration time and time again. Yet in their required assessment much of this honest personal commentary and questioning was held at bay; their efforts focused on the analysis of stylistic devices, a cohesive structure, authentic voice, and varied diction. In an effort to help my students feel successful, I made formulas and how-to sheets to approach these difficult written exams.

It was the end of another heavy school year and I was buried in grading practice papers for the English A: Literature exam. At one point Marien, a diligent, anxious seventeen-year-old, handed me one such paper, then paused and with exhausted urgency inquired, "When will I get this back? Because I need to know the parts that are wrong as soon as possible." And there it was again, my job as teacher: the beholder of what is right and what is wrong. What happened to writing?

Over the course of teaching middle-school and high-school English, I had become repulsed, angered, and disheartened by the purpose writing has taken in school. I was surprised (for a heartbeat) that Applebee's (2000) study of US secondary-school writing found that only 3% of classwork and homework involved writing original text. His depiction of writing closely matched the tasks I assigned my sisters:

> The majority of writing activities in school involved writing without composing: fill in the blank and completion exercises, direct translation, or other seat work in which the text was constructed by the textbook or the teacher, and the student supplied the missing information that was, typically, judged as right or wrong. (p. 90)

It was time to go back to school to learn, again. I applied to graduate school back across the ocean in Minnesota and wrote in my application that I am taking a leave of absence from being the judge of writing to mine the field of narration.

WRITER'S WORKSHOP

When the women in Audrey's group agreed to jump, I looked back on my relationship with writing while straining to look forward. My greatest frustration looking back over my shoulder was that I could see the usefulness and purpose of writing falling short and flat—especially in schools. In its utilization to reproduce knowledge, writing often became inaccessible and unappealing as a tool to affect well-being. When I requested writing in my language-arts or world-literature classroom to move past representation of a grade or course content—to be reflective, narrative, perhaps raw and exposing—it became dangerously, wholly representative of the student or student's experience.

In Tim's class, I started reading Barbara Kamler's *Relocating the Personal*. In her text, she runs a writer's workshop with aging women. In identifying the purpose of her workshop she writes: "The aim is not to reveal the truth of the writer's personal experience or express who they really are [...] it is to understand that in writing subjectivity may be defined, contested, and remade" (Kamler, 2001, p. 61). This purpose provided a new framework to support my strain to look forward. I recognized I believed truth can be revealed, unraveled, and realized in writing; Kamler widened my gaze to consider that the text and writer were in production during writing. I began to contemplate if and how a writer's subjectivity—a conscious and unconscious understanding of her mind and body—can be "defined, contested, and remade" in writing. Could teachers destruct dominant narratives of teacher and teaching and construct new subjectivities through writing? If yes, how?

When planning the writer's workshop for the group of new teachers, I spent considerable amount of time on the invite. Simply asking new teachers to write down their stories was not enough; an invitation was necessary, essential. I turned back to *Writing at the Edge* by Jeff Park. In his Writer's Group at the Canadian Mental Health Association, he called the writing produced by its members "cultural artifacts" (Park, 2005). One member of the group, Albert, discussed how his writing served as a permanent record for others to refer to at any time. Park reframed Albert's cultural artifact as a "site of meaning making" (p. 14). In his construction of his writer's group, the writing existed as artifact, as resource for other writers, as a concrete object to circle round, be in, and derive meaning from. I appreciated this shift in usefulness and purpose; the idea of "cultural artifacts" propelled my gaze forward—seeking other artifacts.

With the teachers in mind, I considered what artifacts would invite writing. I moved beyond text and considered objects, documentation, and photographs. In looking back on my teaching career, I thought about the gum under the tables, the comic strip I taped by my classroom number, the class photo of us hiking (where you can't tell I'm the teacher), and my first teaching contract where I signed my name by the $28,500 yearly salary. I hoped the use of artifacts would invite sustained meaning-making, and I anticipated we would quickly realize they do not exist alone (Pahl & Rowsell, 2010). Artifacts undoubtedly evoked emotion, carried space and time, and represented conflict and new and ignored truths.

~~~

We had agreed to meet at Amanda's house because it was most central. It was June, the middle of the month, when the temperature starts to rise. We—Amanda, Aubrey, Marie, Sam, Audrey, and I—met for three consecutive evenings. I give you our writing workshop overview with the understanding that like any lesson plan, we skipped some parts and overindulged in others. I give you the narration of our time together that summer to understand how this work, the (re)narration of teacher identity, rooted down and bravely grew.

WRITER'S WORKSHOP OVERVIEW:

	Date/Location/Artifacts	Agenda
Part 1: Writer's Workshop	Workshop Day 1: 6/23/15 Location: Amanda's Artifacts: Objects	1. Warm write: Letter Writing, Dear Anna, *What is your relationship with writing?* 2. Artifact write: An interview with an object that represents a struggle 3. Summer overview: artifacts to enable narration, select artifact(s) for your writing project 4. Life graphing: graph first year of teaching, highs low, label academic and personal events 5. Close out: Graph/Workshop Day 1 reflections
	Workshop Day 2: 6/24/15 Location: Amanda's Artifacts: Texts	1. Warm write: "My Name" from *The House on Mango Street*, Name writing and sharing 2. Artifact write: edTPA or classroom observation, expand on selected lines from text 3. Writing project: *How do I select an artifact?* 4. Close out: Share possible writing project ideas
	Workshop Day 3: 6/25/15 Location: Amanda's Artifacts: Photographs	1. Warm write: "Women diapers/Vigina stuffers" photo from Sam's found art 2. Artifact write: Childhood photos, write from perspective of the child you or someone in photo 3. Discussion: *Who narrates your story and why?* 4. Writing project: *What does this artifact say about my teacher identity?* 5. Close out: Writing routines
Part 2: Writing Conferences	Writing + Conferences: 6/26/15-7/23/15 Location: open Artifacts: Individual Selections	1. Conference timeslots (July 7-15) 2. Conversation/feedback/repositioning on writing project *Optional group meeting: July 16 1. Project check-in 2. Sample feedback to writing 3. Prep for retreat
Part 3: Retreat	Retreat: 7/24/15 Location: Cabin Artifacts: Writing Projects	1. Set group norms for retreat 2. Prep sharing of writing projects 3. Discuss possible next steps: reflective practioner, Womens' press, publication, gallery
	Retreat: 7/25/15 Location: Cabin Artifacts: Writing Projects	1. An Intro: How you decided on your artifact/writing project and why it's important to you 2. Sharing: How you would like us to engage with or experience your work (read it out loud, have us read silently, share a part and have us write, etc.) 3. Feedback: How you would like to receive feedback on your work (questions, identifying places where we want to know more, check the *Feedback like Kamler*)

Anna Schick, Writer's Workshop, 2015

Figure 1: Writer's Workshop Curriculum
Source: Author

Writer's Workshop Day 1

Amanda's house sat kitty-corner from the school where she taught. Her husband left with their dog Wally as we gathered at the table. It felt strange to teach teachers. I am usually one of the critics in my graduate classes—always envisioning a better way to design the discussion or provide feedback. I knew they might do the same. Additionally, when we teach we often teach those younger than us. These women were my own age, had haircuts like me, and threw out a "fuck" for good measure every now and then. I had arrived; I was invited to listen to actual voices without later having to rate voice on a scale of 1–5.

The first thing I asked them to do was write me a letter. The objective was to understand their past and present relationship with writing and their goals for our writer's workshop. The format of the letter allowed a personal, non-academic response and an accessible artifact to draw on in the future. Most letters were at least one page's worth of honest, raw prose chronicling a love–hate relationship with writing. These excerpts allow you to hear the teachers themselves:

> My current relationship with writing is that it's something I did in the past. In high school I was a member, and then president of the Creative Writing Club that would meet once a month to share writing. It was a great outlet, and it felt creative. At the time, I was heavily using drugs and alcohol, so there was some of that tragic-drug-addicted-why-is-life-so-hard-for-me attitude going on. (Amanda)

> I am looking forward to exploring my insecurities and areas of growth in my teaching. Writing often feels safer than speaking when uncovering the parts of myself of which I am not proud. (Marie)

> I write when I am embarrassed, guilty, or ashamed. (Aubrey)

> I want to make sense of myself, my work, and my mental health. I want others to see what I see—with a crude/funny tone. (Sam)

Following the letters, we moved to our first artifact exercise. I asked everyone to take out their artifact that represented a struggle. The six of us glanced around Amanda's table topped with MacBooks, notebooks, and real books, and then at each other. *Here we go.* There was so much trust established in this group before I arrived on scene. I better understand, now, how our well-being is dependent on the well-being of others. This collective sitting around the table, with early-summer tans and the first week of rested sleep after a long school year, loved each other. They took genuine interest in each other's lives—and they were strong, strong enough to hear and respond to each other's struggles. I wanted to start here, with an artifact that represented a struggle, because it cracks open the vulnerability and the undeniable humanness in each of us. Before we could talk about what it was like to be teacher, we had to talk about what it means to be human.

Slowly, everyone dug out their artifacts from their bags. Amanda got up and took hers off the shelf in the living room. I asked them to first engage with their artifacts in written dialogue. Sam, sitting to my left, set an orange prescription bottle on her notebook. Aubrey laid a paintbrush alongside her pencil and Marie unfolded fancy embroidery. Audrey positioned her ancient blue cell phone at arm's reach and I laid a pair of clip-on earrings gently on the table. Once there was a sense of readiness, I instructed them to write a question to their artifact, then respond as their artifact, and continue the dialogue until the time was out.

Sam questioned her prescription bottle: "Who are you? And why are you here?" In dialogue, Aubrey's paintbrush challenged: "Why don't you use me anymore?" After a few minutes passed, I asked them to exchange artifacts. Holding someone else's struggle, I asked them to write from the first-person perspective. Amanda held Aubrey's paintbrush and wrote down what she imagined the brush was thinking and feeling. Aubrey picked up Amanda's artifact—a child's menorah, candle holders on the top representing the nights of Hanukkah. Aubrey wrote from the menorah's perspective on the shelf, observing Amanda leave for school and return each day.

After writing, I shared my purpose for talking to inanimate objects. First, it got us in—it cut past the lead-up story to what we struggle with and got us talking directly to the issue. I asked them to trade because I felt it represented our attempt to empathize with or understand each other's struggles—and in doing this, we helped each other to reposition the view on the struggle and perhaps initiate a (re)narration. I also wanted to communicate that, while we can sometimes view each other's struggles and imagine a narration, we never really know until we ask, and more importantly listen. In sharing, we were all surprised by Marie's secret desires to stay home and cross-stitch and knit. We listened to Audrey's honest fears about buying a new smartphone—the easy accessibility to more work and the potential distancing from the important people near her. Sam shares the responses of her Adderall bottle and the exercise's effect in her chapter later on.

After our first go at writing from an artifact, I delved into what I was up to. I passed out a writer's workshop overview and attempted to explain my developing thoughts on why this mattered. I noted how using objects invited us to write; it gave us a literal starting point. Our artifacts carry a narration of their own and being willing to crack this open is a willingness to go deeper, gain new understanding, and consider aspects we keep locked up because of the potential flood damage. I knew, as a teacher myself, that we locked up many parts of ourselves and our daily struggles as teacher in order to keep doing what we do. I also knew that we, as white female teachers, we were artifacts too, with a dominant narration trailing us. I believed in order to keep teaching we needed to crack ourselves open as teachers. I knew this would not be easy, it would not happen overnight, and it would not solve the challenge of teaching—but it would hopefully make us feel less alone and more conscious of our ability to construct our teacher identities. In order to crack open these hard white female shells that presented as teacher, I asked them to consider artifacts that they could use for a writing project about what it means to be a teacher. Some had ideas right away, while others spent the duration of the writer's workshop and beyond locating artifacts and experiences they could use to start this (re)narration.

We ended the first evening session with large A3 sheets of paper and #2 pencils. I asked each teacher to graph the academic year (her first year of teaching), marking events above or below a centered line (Rief, 1992). This was an open map of their first year of classroom events, observation dates, relationship or family highs or lows. We scribbled away silently for fifteen minutes or more. Then, I asked them to share the experience of creating the graph. I followed up with, "Anything surprise you?"

"How many high points I had," Aubrey chimed in immediately. Sam, "Me too." Amanda noted some low points involving tears in front of her students.

Marie lingered at the end of the graph—the high point, the excitement of being offered a new teaching position and the low mark, coming to terms with some of her colleagues' assumptions about her decision to move schools.

We shared family time, winter break trips, the rock bottom points—a best friend with breast cancer, notice of no rehire, the breaking point with that one student we all have. These graphs led us to an important conversation about our teacher experiences spilling into our "private" lives—and how we just wanted one life. Ultimately, these graphs would serve as a reference, an artifact, to examine the intersections of our lives as teacher and person.

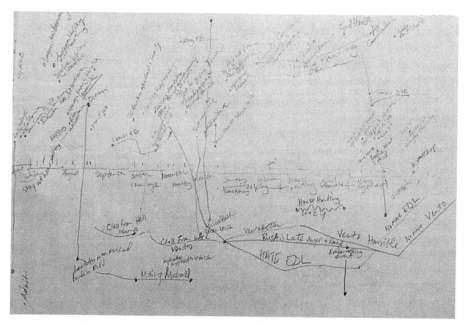

Figure 2: Aubrey's Life Graph
Source: Aubrey Hendry

I left the writer's workshop and drove the thirty minutes home that evening with a strange feeling of full and hungry. This work fed me and left me craving more. I wanted to pick at and peel back the paint and expose the covered-up shades and unsure truths beneath teacher.

Writer's Workshop Day 2

As the wild rice salad made its way around the table, I shared our plan for this evening's writer's workshop. "Tonight we will be thinking about text as artifact." We started with a vignette titled "My Name" from *The House on Mango Street* by

Sandra Cisneros (1984). I asked them to read it silently and underline passages that stood out to them. This was an exercise I had recently experienced as a student in my Social Justice Writing course at the University of Minnesota. After everyone finished, I read the vignette out loud. I asked them to join in wherever they had underlined sections of the text. On some lines, a lone voice from the table joined mine, at other points we created a chorus of bold readers. In the text, Esperanza speaks about the origin and meaning of her name. Early on, she says, "It was my great-grandmother's name and now it is mine." (10) As I read further, all the women's voices spoke up and loudly read, "a wild horse of woman, so wild she wouldn't marry. Until my great-grandfather threw a sack over her head and carried her off. Just like that, as if she was a fancy chandelier." (11) There was a pause before I continued reading; we looked up from our text for a quick smile at each other. I was surprised at the unity I felt in their voices joining mine and the power when every voice chose to be heard. When we finished the excerpt, I asked them how it felt to read like this. They recalled the points where we all chimed in, including "the wild horse of woman." Audrey told a story about her grandmother, another wild horse. Sam started googling the lyrics to a Bob Dylan song. We concluded—*we* are wild horses. What this means to each teacher is different but in so many ways we are all wild and strong and sturdy yet feel corralled and reigned in and weighted down.

In a similar fashion to Esperanza, I asked each teacher to write about their name. Sam is called Ms. Scott and Marie is Marie in a Montessori school. Amanda spoke *to* her name: "I abandoned you the minute I signed my teacher contract." We paused to consider what else we abandoned.

We talked about students' names. I recalled what it felt like to read the roster of my first class. My tongue silently curling each name. Talking about names led to talking about humanness—this murky abyss that fills in the frames of teachers and students. Names our parents and partners call us brought hearty laughter and flashes of our personal, private selves to the table. The truth emerged that Aubrey was named after a song by the band Bread. We also noted the range of names we are called in schools, including bitch, racist, Ma'am, and the slip of Mom every now and then.

This name exercise was practice for cracking open text, granting permission to approach and recraft the memories and emotions trapped in words. We took a break to refill water, put plates in the dishwasher, take bathroom breaks. Once resettled, I asked them to take out their teaching observations. Like reading the text from *The House on Mango Street*, I asked them to underline sections from their observations or edTPA where they wanted to respond, question, or crack open.

Aubrey read aloud comments she underlined in her observation: "You did not clearly articulate […] the goal was not clearly attached." (If there was a voice I could insert into this text for you to hear, it would be Aubrey's. I wish there was a button right here you could push like in a children's book and suddenly you would perk up as you hear Aubrey's animated, quick and questioning voice—one that inevitably makes all us Wild Horses think harder and laugh louder). She responded to this underlined feedback:

> This is the part I don't like to do because it is so hard to talk in kid language. This seems to align with the idea that kids are little adults. This doesn't match my philosophy but I can do it and then I'm successful…but…

She admitted that this feedback made her feel defensive and embarrassed. She questioned how much she would allow her worth as teacher to be defined by the comments and marks on this rubric. Then Marie brought up that she underlined learning targets—the floodgates opened and suddenly we were all talking at once. One by one, we shut up because Sam's stories are the best and she had one to share:

> For two weeks I didn't change my learning target. Someone wrote on the board, "Eat Pie," I thought it was fucking hilarious. So I left it…and it was up during one of my observations. I just stopped caring and I stopped trying.

> I want kids to write funny shit on my walls. How do I fight the system? And how do I keep a job? I have to work. Teaching is a lifestyle and it affects every moment of my life…I am never going to fit a mold.

The conservation ebbed and flowed. We talked about objectives. About observations being subjective. About how we crave feedback and support, yet evaluations and classrooms observations make us sweaty and anxious like we're onstage and we forgot the lines.

As we cracked open our teaching observations, we started to crack open our teacher identities. The writing in response to lines of feedback or critique raised up a serious and large conversation about how to be human *and* be teacher. What parts of ourselves do we shut down to teach? Every time we give middle-schoolers a serious face when the topic of poop is raised rather than laughing with them, our humanness diminishes a little more. Every time we stop a kindergartener from dancing in the hallway in an effort to the show the other teachers *we take walking in the hallway seriously*, we wonder what school is really all about. When the tears well because fifth-graders won't be quiet and control is seemingly slipping through our fingers, we swallow the emotion and conjure up the badass-bitch-I-don't-take-no-shit face and announce that recess is a privilege and you just lost it.

We ended here for the evening. I believed we felt exhausted but healthy, like finishing a run in the summer heat. I reminded the group about bringing in childhood photos tomorrow. Getting in my car that night, I remembered sorting through this mix of shock and excitement—it was working. We were digging beneath and listening and repositioning and shouting loud and crying and laughing. This happens often when wild women gather around a table—if only these tables existed more often in teacher education and inside schools.

Writer's Workshop Day 3

As you can imagine by now, this wasn't the last time we met. Almost a year after this workshop, we took time to reflect back on these three days. Amanda wrote:

> I loved being the host during this. Like, opening my home to this beautiful and pure purpose. It's a cliché but it made my house feel like a home. Probably on the third night, it all felt natural, like we'd been together all along. Good food, laughing, crying, feeling vulnerable. The start of something new and exciting.

I felt it too. There was an ease and natural sense about us all working together. When you make a choice that then feels necessary, you know you chose well.

On the third evening, I started talking about questions I knew were drifting about: "What now?" "Where do we go from here?" "That's nice that we did some talking and writing, but so what?" "Do we have 'assignments' and 'deadlines?'" I explained that (if they wanted) each person would choose an artifact or experience that they can use to start cracking open their teacher identity. Looking around, I asked if anyone had ideas so far. The awkward silence followed, as it often does in a classroom when a teacher waits for a volunteer. I gave it a heartbeat or two and then Sam spoke from the living room. She was taking pictures of the brownies I brought for the group. With fresh excitement over our new name, I used white tubed frosting and wrote *Wild Horses* on baked brownies. This warm, boxed baked good quickly became a refuge in upcoming meetings. She said, "I'm already collecting artifacts." Sam had been documenting bathroom graffiti, scribbles on walls, and other raw messages from students. Amanda chimed in that she was considering writing haikus about experiences in her first year but wasn't sure yet. I did not want to choose these projects for them—they were theirs. We had scheduled a retreat a month from now to share our work, and conferences with me in between.

Returning to our evening agenda, tonight our work was with photos as artifacts. Everyone laid their family pictures out on the table or located them in their phones. We ran through a "Perceive" exercise, noting what we noticed in the picture, what we felt, what it reminded us of, and what questions we had (Weismann Art Museum, 2005). Following this, I asked everyone to choose a person in the picture and write from his, her, or their perspective. After writing and sharing, we shifted our focus from family photos to the first year teaching graphs produced during Writer's Workshop Day 1. I asked them to locate a mark on their graph that happened in their classroom and make a snapshot of the event in their head. Then, they wrote from the perspective of a student in the snapshot. This writing was hard because it forced us away from the comfort and security of our vantage point to take up another, and thereby repositioned our take on—and control of—the situation. From here, we were able to tell (and understand) the story differently. This exercise with photos as artifacts eventually led into Aubrey's unique work with scripts in an upcoming chapter.

WRITING PROJECTS

For teachers, summer is a fleeting oasis. We cringe every time we hear, "Oh, you're a teacher—it must be so nice to have your summers off!" But for many of us, our summers are haunted. Our students, colleagues, and classrooms show up in our dreams. Target brings out the back-to-school dollar section a good month too early. A new school year offers up both hope and an expectation for a better year. In this restoration period, we are drawn to work on all the parts we wish were better during the school year: teachers imagine new approaches to social justice, seek out new resources, and dream about this year being the year they keep their well-being in check.

Our summer workshop tip-toed this line of *work*. I didn't want to create extra work for these women. But I heard their reflections and stories and knew in writing their subjectivity could be redefined. There was a disconnection between who they *thought* they should be as teachers and who they really *were*. It was difficult to write about this because it is not easy to tell stories outside of the dominant narrative of teaching. I believed that to interrupt the dominant narrative of a teacher as a stressed out, underpaid savior—or conversely, a sweet white woman with construction paper and a rug for story time—we needed to start telling truths about teaching. These dominant narratives hurt us; and we need to rewrite teaching stories in ways that are more generous, critical, and honest. Writing about the deep humanness in teaching is important for re-imagining and diversifying the teaching profession; for our collective well-being; for our practices; and for our students.

Following our three-day writer's workshop, I met up with each teacher individually to talk about their writing. I met Sam at Blue Moon Coffee Shop. When she arrived she handed me a small bag. Inside was a coffee mug with a watercolor painting of a horse—Wild Horses.

After we ordered coffee, Sam pulled out a stack of images. Small square photos of penis drawings in green sharpie, permanent marker in the hallway, pencil scribbles scratching out the work of the previous artist, full conversations blooming on bathroom stalls. We sorted them in piles—photos with the words "bitch," "fuck," and "deez nuts" each had their own pile.

We got to talking about who writes these messages and why—who erases or cleans them away and why. We drew a concentric circle in response to the question, "Whose space is it anyway?"

As a teacher of writers, I was developing a greater self-consciousness about how narratives are made and how they can be written differently (Kamler, 2001). Sam could easily write about graffiti as vandalization; she could write about how we need the Arts back in schools; she could talk about students' lack of respect; or she could ignore it, like most teachers, and let the janitor scrub it from the bathroom wall. Or she could craft a narrative about humor and space and mental health interrupting the dominant narrative of teachers, students, and schools.

Kamler (2001) reminds us, "Without [these new narratives] none of us has any way of gaining enough distance to make dominant [narratives] visible and thereby to imagine alternatives. And most educational and policy contexts are badly in need of new stories and real alternatives" (p. 77). Writing from artifacts enabled teachers to reposition and retell narratives of teaching. (Re)narration both acknowledges and interrupts dominant narrations.

Aubrey came bouncing into the Blue Moon Coffee Shop after Sam. She decided to take mental snapshots of difficult situations with students (similar to what we did with our life graph) and write scripts from the students' perspectives. I asked her to read all her scripts out loud—which I loved because she went into her lively, animated four-year old voice. I asked her why she chose these situations and this led us into a rich conversation questioning control in the classroom. This writing repositioned her teacher view by taking up a student perspective. Through writing she considered how much control she really has—and how much is really needed—and what she could be missing in the effort to be in control.

(RE)NARRATION

A month after our writer's workshop, we arrived in the real heat of the summer. In the middle of July, I invited Audrey and the teachers to a small cabin for a retreat. Between cool dips in the lake, we shared our writing projects. We didn't have a plan—we didn't know where this writing and sharing would take us but we trusted it was good.

They all wrote; I wrote too. Through our summer workshop, I came to know (re)narrating as repositioning your view on your story and telling it again. And again. The artifacts and collective enabled (re)narration; they repositioned teacher and teaching again and again. The use of the artifacts—text messages, embroidery, snapshots of students, and graffiti—gave the cracking a starting place. If we want to break apart and reimagine teacher identity, where to begin could be so daunting the task never gets started. The writing produced during the writer's workshop went on to serve as new artifacts for the collective. These artifacts were resources representing more than an individual story; they represented social, political, and cultural contexts of education. They saw themselves in each other's stories; they heard alternative ways to be and become teacher; they challenged the narration a fellow teacher had assigned herself; they called out disregarded emotion or down-played struggles. The collective's response to each teacher's writing repositioned the teacher, suggested new ways to view teacher identity, and gave her strength and safety to (re)narrate the story again.

They had spent so much of their time during their first months of teaching suiting up and keeping it together, it felt refreshing to let it all unravel and get honest. The writing was unpolished, uncomfortable, and truthful. This was not easy—to ask teachers to write about what is current, what is real, and what is raw. It is not easy peel off the teacher identity you imagine you should have and under-stand the one that is.

In writing their chapters, the teachers take up and recraft their subjectivity. They are imagining new ways to be teacher. They are giving up on the static story of teacher and repositioning their views on their teacher [well] being. Their stories are in no way complete—they are partial and in progress. As all of our stories are. I invite you to listen in on their experience in the classroom, in the writer's work-shop, in the collective, and especially, in their bodies and minds as teacher.

REFERENCES:

Applebee, A. (2000). Alternative models of writing development. In R. Indrisano. & J.R. Squire (Eds). *Perspectives on Writing: Research, Theory, and Practice* (90–110). Newark, Delaware: International Reading Association.

Cisnesos, S. (2009). *The House on Mango Street.* New York, NY: Vintage Books.

Kamler, B. (2001). *Relocating the Personal: A Critical Writing Pedagogy.* Albany, NY: SUNY Press.

Pahl, K. & Rowsell, J. (2010). *Artifactual Literacies: Every Object Tells a Story.* New York, NY: Teachers College Press.

Park, J. (2005). *Writing at the Edge: Narrative and Writing Process Theory.* (Vol. 248). New York, NY: Peter Lang.

Petkau, et al. (2005). *Artful Writing: A Resource for Teachers.* Minneapolis, MN: Weisman Art Museum.

Rief, L. (1992). *Seeking Diversity: Language Arts with Adolescents.* Portsmouth, NH: Heinemann Educational Books.

CHAPTER THREE

Human/Teacher

BY AMANDA MOHAN

SENSITIVE

You're so sensitive.

My mom called me "sensitive" when I was a kid. I was sensitive because I couldn't spend the night at a friend's house without being homesick and crying through the night. In second grade, Nora invited me for a sleepover at her house. We made cupcakes and ate pizza for dinner. At bedtime, Nora fell asleep immediately, which left me alone with my thoughts in her canopy bed. I decided the best course of action would be to have my parents pick me up. At 10 p.m., I tiptoed out of Nora's room in my Care Bears nightgown and into the living room, where her parents were watching TV, and proclaimed that I needed to call my parents and go home, followed by an outpouring of tears. Nora's mom looked at the clock and told me, in her kindest voice, that it was too late for them to pick me up. My seven-year-old brain detected imminent danger and a loss of control, and my crying turned into sobbing as I gasped for air. Completely powerless and not sure how to use a phone by myself, I accepted Nora's mom's offer to sit with her on the couch. For what felt like hours, I continued to cry and ask to call my parents, but my requests were denied and met with more back rubs. The night would eventually end, but in my anxiety-ridden head, I was convinced it wouldn't. Anxiety and depression are like that, and I would continue to experience whole days and weeks of being unable to see beyond my own thoughts, well into adulthood.

You're so sensitive.

I was sensitive because I convinced myself my parents would get into a wreck, plane crash, etc. every time they left the house. I was sensitive because I projected feelings onto inanimate objects like shampoo bottles, pencils, and dirty clothes on the floor. Everything needed to be touching something else so it wouldn't be lonely. It took me an extra ten minutes to leave my bedroom or bathroom each day since I needed to relieve the loneliness in all of my possessions.

You're so sensitive.

I was sensitive because I had my first panic attack in 1993 when I was eight years old, attending the same private school in Atlanta where my three older sisters went before me. In third grade we took a standardized test, the Educational Records Bureau (ERB). My teacher, Ms. Anderson, assured the class that while we needed to try our *very best*, the test was only to see how our school was doing compared to other schools. Days before the test, Ms. Anderson had us practice bubbling in our names using fake Scantron sheets with newly sharpened #2 pencils.

The first day of testing arrived. I put on the same uniform—a khaki jumper and light blue button-down shirt—I had worn the day before, along with a pair of navy blue shorts to wear under my jumper in case my skirt flew up during recess. I ate a piece of toast with peanut butter and honey in the car with my dad and sister. He dropped us off at our respective schools—I at the elementary wing, and my sister at the middle school. I was greeted by a staff member in the carpool line and walked down the hallway to my classroom. But, instead of walking inside and hanging up my book bag as I usually did, I froze. It was as if someone had changed the channel, and when the channel changed I was no longer in control. My body stayed there, but my mind left.

After a few seconds, I walked away from my classroom toward the office. Maybe I was going there to call my mom and ask her to pick me up, or just to be somewhere else, anywhere that was not in front of the students in my class. Halfway to the office, the guidance counselor, Ms. Greenwood, stopped to ask me where I was going. I burst into tears as I opened my mouth to tell her, "I can't. I can't. I can't." She steered me into her office and pushed a box of tissues my way as I collapsed into the chair by her desk. I proceeded to tell her that the rest of my class was taking the ERB, but that I couldn't. At the time I didn't have words to describe what I was experiencing. All I could do was cry and say "I can't."

She left me in her office while she checked in with my teacher, Ms. Anderson, and then she kept me company in her office for the rest of that day's testing. I played with various items in her office and read books while I waited for the rest of my class to finish their tests. Once the class was done, Ms. Greenwood sent me back to my classroom and I finished my day, resolved to take the test with the other students tomorrow.

The next day came, and instead of making it into my classroom, I went straight to Ms. Greenwood's office because my little third-grade brain had changed the channel again: I still couldn't make it into my classroom. I ended up sitting at Ms. Greenwood's desk, taking the test on my own that day. I recall thinking to myself, "Hey, this isn't so bad," and immediately feeling embarrassed about my emotional display.

More than Sensitive

At age 13, I visited a therapist after admitting to my mom that I had scary, intrusive thoughts, like grabbing the steering wheel and driving us off the road every time I sat in the front seat of the car. The therapist turned my label of "sensitive" into generalized anxiety disorder. Being assigned a label brought me some kind of relief, but it did nothing to curb the anxiety. Anti-anxiety medication took the edge off, but I still wasn't in control.

A couple years later, as the anxiety and panic attacks stayed with me, I discovered that recreational drugs and drinking worked far better than my prescribed medication. I called it *self*-medicating.

Eventually, by 18, I lost control, as addicts and alcoholics often do. The scary, intrusive car-crash thoughts returned, but I was no longer the passenger; I was the driver, and each tree I passed looked like the one that could help me end it. In January 2004, I ended up at a treatment center in Rochester, Minnesota for a five-month stay. After that, I always considered my first year of recovery the most difficult year of my life—until I became a teacher.

WILD HORSES

The Group

The first time we met at Audrey's table in 2013, I was incredibly nervous. Audrey was my favorite, most memorable professor at Augsburg, and now she'd invited me into her home because she felt I had something to contribute. As she mentions in this book's introduction, our group originated because she sensed in us a "desire for more connection, perhaps outside of the confines of a classroom and 'official' work, for collective dialogue and companionship" (January 2013).

I jumped at this opportunity because no matter how caring, open, or compassionate a person (for instance, my husband) might be, the only one who can truly understand a teacher's situation is a fellow teacher. But back then I wasn't even a teacher yet, and it felt almost impossible to begin the task of becoming one. We sat at the large table, petted Audrey's dog, met her two daughters and her husband, drank tea, wrote, and talked. During our first few meetings, I stole glances at the books on Audrey's shelves by the table, titles like *Women's Bodies, Women's Wisdom, Their Eyes were Watching God,* and *Beloved,* alongside a variety of science fiction novels. I wanted to know what a proud, reflective, feminist professor of teachers read and thought about in her spare time.

I don't recall many specific details of that first meeting, but Audrey recorded our conversations and kept brief notes about each one. She eventually had someone transcribe a few of them. In the transcript of our third meeting together, we began by going around the table and stating our reasons for being there. I said:

> I'm Amanda and definitely to [have] a sense of community. I like being a part of, and it's a way to continue, you know, you have discussions in class like especially in this last class with Audrey, but you only have that limited amount of time so you kinda wanna delve deeper and I think that's what this is good for. (March 2013)

This reason for being in The Group is still true three years later. Every now and then, I'm reminded that not all teachers have this type of support and community that I've grown accustomed to. One such reminder came when The Group presented at the *Journal of Language & Literacy Education* (*JoLLE*) conference at the University of Georgia in Athens, Georgia. I initially felt like sharing my work with people outside of The Group didn't make a lot of sense. The Group knew me, knew my struggles, knew me well. The audience members at the conference had never seen me before. Why would they care? But they did, because The Group isn't special in our confusion and frustration with the teaching profession. Teachers and teacher educators in the audience thanked us, sometimes with tears in their eyes, for being so honest and opening a dialogue about teachers' well-being. When sj asked us to write this book, sj hammered home the idea that teachers besides us could benefit from hearing our story.

During the fourth session of The Group, in April of 2013, Audrey wanted to get to know us better, so she asked us to write about turning points in our lives. The idea came from her daughter Noa, who'd been given the same writing assignment in school. In the moment, we laughed, wondering how anything in a thirteen-year-old's life could be important enough to qualify as a turning point. I cringe when I revisit my response in the transcript, because until I started teaching—like, had *my own classroom*—I didn't see or notice or understand the complexity of childhood in the students I interacted with every day. I didn't even notice the complexity of my own childhood and its anxiety-riddled turning points, beginning with my long night at Nora's house.

We took a few minutes to write about turning points on our own. I remember I hovered my pen above my notebook, and saw out of the corner of my eye that everyone else was furiously writing. It was the same feeling I'd get in grade school when the teacher would ask a question or post something on the board for us to write about, and then everyone in the class (or so it seemed) got right to work while I had no fucking clue what was going on. At the table that night, it ultimately didn't matter what I wrote, because I opened up to The Group and told them about my history with drug and alcohol abuse, depression, and anxiety. Audrey then shared her own experience with anxiety and depression. Then she said, "I won't force anyone else to say anything, but I think you're in good company," and the entire table erupted in laughter. One by one we took turns divulging our histories of therapy, medication, anxiety and depression. Some of The Group had lived their entire lives with it; others had meltdowns later, in college and grad school. I was certainly in good company. The themes of mental health and well-being would carry us throughout our many meetings, right up to the day we met Anna, and beyond.

(RE)NARRATING

Using Text Messages as Artifacts

During the first two years of The Group's existence, we hadn't done a lot of writing. Anna's arrival gave us a new energy to express ourselves in writing, as well as the new name Wild Horses. Anna introduced the concept of writing using artifacts. On the first day of our three-day writing workshop, we created a Life Graph[1] about our last year of teaching, rating the quality of our experiences over time. Above a horizontal line we placed our positive experiences (the higher the better) and below the line our negative ones. Then we connected the dots to make zig-zag graphs of the last twelve months. There were a lot of ups and downs, but once I finally had my own classroom, mostly downs.

I didn't have to interview for the position, since I'd already worked in the same K-8 Minneapolis school for the previous three years as an Assistant Educator. As I was finishing my student teaching at a different school across town, friends of mine who worked at my old school told me to apply for the fifth-grade English language arts/social studies position because Victoria, its current inhabitant, was, um, not working out so well. She resigned at the end of the fall semester, effectively abandoning her students. After accepting the position, I went to meet Victoria and see the classroom I'd be taking over. The first thing I noticed was the floor: the institutional linoleum tile was covered in blackish-grey marks and trash. Victoria explained that the engineer had stopped cleaning her room a couple weeks ago.

I'd later learn that the engineer refused to clean classroom floors unless the chairs were stacked, and that was something Victoria wouldn't or couldn't convince the kids to do on a daily basis.

I was filled with judgment. How difficult could it be to have students stack their own chairs or clean the area around their desks? But not long after I took over the classroom I realized why a teacher might stop asking kids to stack chairs or walk in line: The time it takes to actually get them accustomed to doing the things you want them to do feels excessive. I reviewed the procedure for leaving the room several times with my students; there's a PowerPoint slide on the board with clip art and arrows and a "fun" font that lays out each step of the process to stack your chair, get your backpack, and return to the room where you get in line order and wait for the rest of the class to be done. It seemed like such a simple process, one that shouldn't be a teacher's breaking point, but it was just too much. It was too much because I'd taught them this already, I wanted them to be better, so therefore they *should* be better. It was too much in addition to everything else I was asked to accomplish, which was itself too much. As I made the students return to their seats for a second time in order to redo the tasks because someone didn't do them correctly, I wanted to shout at them, "THIS ISN'T IMPORTANT! Why can't you see that?! This is only to get you safely from one place to the other. This isn't what I want to be teaching you. *This isn't teaching!*" In those moments, I was confronted with the difference between the teacher I wanted to be and the teacher I needed to be. Maybe Victoria quit because she wasn't willing to compromise the former in order to become the latter.

I made it through the first six months of my teaching and finished the year. But only a couple weeks into summer vacation, during the Wild Horses' three-day workshop at my house, I was already terrified about teaching again in August. On the final day of the workshop, Anna asked us to choose an artifact to write about in order to crack open our teacher identity. At first I wanted to write haikus because they're concise, and I love the drama they contain in 17 syllables. I also wanted to avoid droning on about my feelings like I had done so many times before with the Wild Horses. I was determined to make this writing process less about how shitty my experiences had been, and more about how I could recover and prepare for the following school year. The first step was to reconnect with the emotions and trauma of those six months I'd been trying to let go. Here's an example of what my first haiku probably would have looked like:

This year sucked so much
Why does anyone do this job?
Smile for next year

At that point, I couldn't remember many specific details of my teaching experience, but I could still feel the anxiety in the pit of my stomach. Then I remembered that during those six months, I had sent out several S.O.S. text messages to two friends of mine who worked in the building. Neither of them was tied down to a specific classroom, so they would often drop into mine to see how things were going. I realized that revisiting our text correspondences would provide insight into specific, difficult situations, and material for my haikus.

After a few days of digging through our text conversations, I saw that the messages and accompanying emojis told their own stories. My direct back-and-forth dialogues with people were themselves more powerful, more purposeful than any haiku I could make with them. I also couldn't deny the depth the emojis added as I attempted to narrate those six months of teaching. I saw a pattern in these artifacts, especially in my exchanges with my husband. My texts were short, and usually punctuated by an emoji or two, as were his. I was confused when I first re-read these messages, because I was always feeling *so much* during the school day, but the artifacts didn't reflect this. They were short, concise. That's when I decided, with the help of the Wild Horses, to explore what's *beneath* this form of communication.

After I found these artifacts, I took screenshots of conversations where I narrated my day at school. I began to narrate those first six months of teaching. With the Wild Horses and within my writing I took up alternative explanations and different perspectives. When I looked beneath some of my short messages and emojis, I realized that teaching was the hardest thing I had ever done—on par with going to rehab and getting sober; the raw feelings I masked with drugs and alcohol were being masked by the identity of teacher.

In the next section, I present my artifacts—screenshots of text messages—followed by my original narration that I shared with the Wild Horses at our cabin retreat. The original narration was my first attempt to break open these artifacts and understand myself as teacher. After the original narration in italics, I include my current understanding, or (re)narration, of the artifacts.

Artifact 1: The Hardest Thing(s) I've Ever Done

This is the first text exchange I had with my husband (his messages are on the left and mine are on the right) after taking over the fifth-grade classroom in December 2014. Up until my first teaching job, the hardest thing I ever did was leave my family and friends, and move to a state I couldn't identify on a map, to get sober.

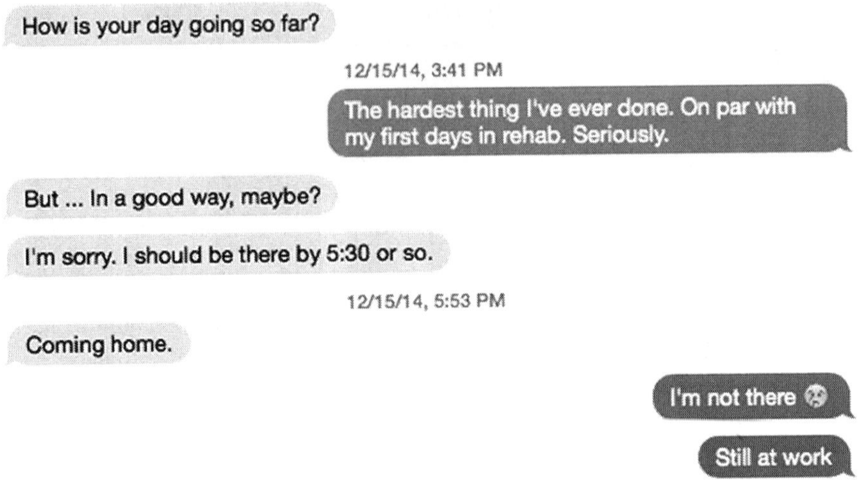

How is your day going so far?

12/15/14, 3:41 PM

The hardest thing I've ever done. On par with my first days in rehab. Seriously.

But ... In a good way, maybe?

I'm sorry. I should be there by 5:30 or so.

12/15/14, 5:53 PM

Coming home.

I'm not there 😣

Still at work

Figure 1: The Hardest Thing(s) I've Ever Done
Source: Author

It was January 2004, and I don't remember the plane ride and subsequent drive to the treatment center in Rochester from the Minneapolis-St. Paul Airport. My parents say I slept most of the way. I wonder if there was snow on the ground, it being January in Minnesota. My parents had never driven in snow before. I bet the roads were clear. For lunch we stopped at a truck stop in Cannon Falls. I wonder what we ate, or if we spoke to each other at all. I remember arriving at The Gables at night, adult women milling around the place, slyly checking out the new arrival. Did I say goodbye to my parents right then and there? Did I stall? Did I beg them not to leave me?

Back then, over ten years ago, I dealt with emotions (positive and negative) in a very different way than I do now. Now I feeeeeeel them. Back then I pushed them beneath the surface by getting high, and needed to stay high to keep the emotions at bay.

During my first months of sobriety, I questioned everything I thought I knew about myself. There was a scene in the Showtime series *Nurse Jackie* that perfectly illustrated the crisis I had shortly after getting sober. A newly sober Jackie, known for not giving a shit about what other people (especially the doctors she worked with) think, showed up in her coworker's office in a panic. Her coworker asked her what's wrong, and Jackie burst into tears and said "Coop doesn't like my hair!"

One of the first things my counselor told me in treatment was that I exhibited a pattern of codependent behavior. She gave me a copy of Melody Beattie's *Codependent No More* (1986). Almost immediately, I saw the error of my ways: my worth, my ability, my contributions to life all depended on what (insert name of whoever happened to be in close proximity to me at the moment) thought of me. It helped me understand my anxiety and sensitivity as a child.

In *Codependent No More*, Beattie writes, "We Are Lovable even if the most important person in your world rejects you, you are still real, and you are still okay." This yearning for acceptance controlled everything I did for the first eighteen years of my life. Once I found out about this "character defect," as my counselor called it, it didn't vanish, not even a little bit. If I was going to stay sober, I needed to develop self-worth and independence. I learned about myself in the context of my addiction, giving up old behaviors and the intense desire to make everyone around me happy. What I figured out is that even if I make you okay, I'm still not okay.

Throughout my sobriety, there have been a lot of firsts: My first time doing something without being drunk or high. For instance, the first job I had after treatment felt *really* hard. What excuse would I have for showing up late? How was I going to get through the day without sneaking a bump of coke in the middle of my shift? How was I going to be like everybody else? Eventually, I got through those firsts because they were followed by a certain reassuring consistency that wasn't there before; what was once a first became just another part of my routine.

But teaching was different, and consistent is the last word I would use to describe my experience. In my late twenties, armed with a teaching license, standing in front of a classroom of ten- and eleven-year-olds, all my old insecurities came flooding back.

Artifacts 2 & 3: Shitty Days and Pretty Good Days

Having my own classroom was a first that wasn't consistent or easy to navigate. When I looked back at the text message artifacts, I realized I had developed a codependent relationship with the actions and reactions of my students. This was evidenced in the next two exchanges with my husband while he was out of town:

How'd it go today?

1/12/15, 2:48 PM

Shitty. Fuckers. All of them.

Figure 2: Shitty Day
Source: Author

And the next day:

That's wonderful.

That's you after a tough day of teaching, like "ain't no thang"

1/13/15, 4:45 PM

Today was pretty good, and that's how I feel.

Good!

Figure 3: Pretty Good Day
Source: Author

In the first exchange, shitty was my day, [because] fuckers were my students. In the second exchange, the following day, Jake sent me an encouraging kitty image, which matched how I felt. The day was good and I felt good. What surprised me in returning to these text messages that these were back-to-back days in teaching—for me it became clear that my mood was dependent upon my students on a day-to-day basis. I moved toward clarity about why this all was so hard: good students = I'm in control = good day, while naughty students = I'm not in control = bad day.

Well, fuck. I'd spent years examining my relationships with significant others and family members to try and eliminate my codependent tendencies, and now there were another 55 humans with whom I was codependent. It was a roller-coaster of emotions as I tried to navigate the classroom and students each day.

My first year in recovery, I obsessed over the "why?" of being a drug addict and alcoholic. I wanted to find where it all came from. I wanted to be able to look at a particular moment in my life and realize, "Oh! That's where it all went wrong." If I knew what had happened that led me to drink and use drugs, then I could allow myself to move forward, or at least blame someone else—or myself. I ended up asking the same "why?" about my teaching and emotional responses to the students. I hoped that if I could scrutinize the past six months like I had my drinking and drug use, then I wouldn't make the same mistakes the following year. Revisiting my text messages started out as a way to see where I went wrong as a teacher, or what made me so upset, but they ended up being more of an insight into my well-being and the old patterns I had been reliving.

Artifact 4: I'm a Wreck

I continued to examine my text messages from my first six months of teaching during and after the writer's workshop. I realized that the new insights I had into my teaching experiences were not just personal but shared by the Wild Horses too. I wasn't alone. Artifact 4 is part of an exchange between me and a colleague. She was hoping I would join her and other teachers at happy hour after school.

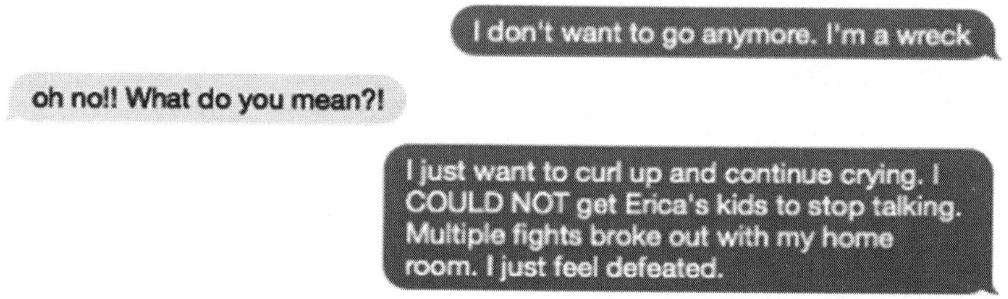

> I don't want to go anymore. I'm a wreck

> oh no!! What do you mean?!

> I just want to curl up and continue crying. I COULD NOT get Erica's kids to stop talking. Multiple fights broke out with my home room. I just feel defeated.

Figure 4: I'm a Wreck
Source: Author

I'm a wreck.

I'm a wreck because no one told me it would be like this: "difficult," "hard," "stressful."
Would they use those same words as I lock my classroom door, turn out the light, and sob

with my head down on the kidney table? But how could they prepare me? My words, even now, don't do the feeling justice.

I'm a wreck because it's Friday and I'm a wreck. This means I dread Friday night, because it comes before Saturday, and Saturday comes before Sunday, and Sunday…. There's no relief because Monday always comes.

I'm a wreck because if my head had been turned ninety degrees to the right, maybe Justin wouldn't have thrown the dictionary, the largest book on the shelf he could grab at a moment's notice, at Abdirahman. And Abdirahman might not have picked up his chair and launched it at Justin. It all could have been avoided. Maybe.

I'm a wreck because Erica's students wouldn't stop talking. I'm a wreck because I'm the teacher. Isn't this my job? Do the students know I can't do my job? Am I turning red yet?

I'm a wreck because I don't want to go to happy hour and complain. Again. Of course my job is hard. All our jobs are hard. All our jobs are the same. I don't need pity or reassurance. I don't know what I need.

I'm a wreck.

Later, at the cabin retreat, I gave everyone a copy of the text messages and my writing about what's beneath "I'm a wreck." I read my work aloud as they followed along. The following is an excerpt of a recorded conversation about my work. I share it here because if Marie can feel like a wreck, then these kinds of experiences weren't mine alone.

Marie: What strikes me about this is how universal the feelings are and after reading yours, holy shit, what the hell am I doing because I'm a wreck. All year long I have to battle against being a wreck. There are always moments that you feel great and things go well but I feel like my underlying current of teaching is that I'm a wreck and I'm always trying to find ways to not be but it's really hard work.

Anna: Why is it universal? Why are all these feelings so closely attached to teaching?

Marie: I think a huge part of it is the institution. You were talking about how there are so many things in place that work against the kind of teachers we want to be or the way that we see teaching. You can blame all sorts of things. It's a really hard job but it's just being made harder by all the things that are put on us, all that you have to live up to and you have to be perfect and you have to get everything in and you have to get everything taught in the year. And you're working with humans. I have children in front of me and they bring just as much to the table as I do.

Me: Obviously we're not crazy, if these feelings are universal, then something's broken.

Marie: We shouldn't be questioning why we decided to become teachers in less than two years. That's why everybody's leaving.

Marie, the type of teacher that I envy—the one that appears to know exactly what she's doing inside her tidy classroom—shared that she too felt like a wreck. Anna asked why the feeling of being a wreck is attached to teaching, or seems to a universal teacher feeling, and Marie replied by stating all the impossible expectations that are put upon teachers in the midst of the difficult task of teaching 30 individual humans at the same time.

This conversation awakened me because Marie, someone that was destined to be a teacher (you'll get a chance to see her extensive family tree of educators in Chapter 5) felt the same way as me. In that moment, I was no longer alone, and if Marie felt that way, then there must be more of us out there. It was the same feeling I got when I realized I was simply an alcoholic and addict or that I had general anxiety disorder—the feeling that you're not crazy, nor are you alone.

Figure 5: Teardrop Emoji
Source: Author

Artifact 5

In artifact 5, I told my husband, Jake, how much my paycheck would be each pay-period, and his response was to send me a bunch of dollar sign emojis (definitely a joke). The next day he sent me a congratulatory text for finishing another week. Jake was using his own words and emojis to re-narrate what I'm saying. Like I ended up doing, he looked beneath the simple texts I sent and interpreted them back to me. That day the checkmark, calendar, pencil, notebook, and microscope did not equal teaching for me. Instead, it was the teardrop emoji.

$1,323.20 after taxes

Nice. $ $ $ $ $ $ $

1/9/15, 4:47 PM

Congratulations on completing another week of teaching! ✓

Thank you. Today was really hard 😣

I'm sorry babe. Want me to call in a bit?

Figure 6: Crybaby
Source: Author

I remember when Mohamed called me a crybaby because I was shocked and embarrassed and afraid. This kid. This ten-year-old kid had figured me out and there was nothing I could do about it because he was my student and I had to carry on with the rest of the class. Mohamed telling the class that I don't wash my hands after picking up dog poop, or that I have AIDS, didn't trigger the same visceral, nauseous feeling because those statements weren't true. But he was right this time: I *am* a crybaby.

I shared the crybaby artifact and story at our cabin retreat. In our conversation, I realized we shared a collective narrative around what it feels like to be teacher and human:

Aubrey: Why do we have to be perfect? I hate that. It directly impacts their future. Every fucking second of the day is like, if I don't do it right, I might screw them up. I hate it. I hate it. I hate it.
Anna: Who says you have to hold it together?
Me: You *do!*
Aubrey: You have to be perfect.
Sam: You can't show emotion.
Me: I'm in the wrong profession.
Anna: Or the profession's wrong.

In the recording of this conversation, when Anna asked, "Who says you have to hold it together?" I practically shouted, "You *do!*" I can see myself throwing up my hands in that moment and letting them crash down onto my thighs, exasperated with this fact. When the other women agreed with me about the need to be perfect and show no emotion, I threw up my hands again and proclaimed that I was in the wrong profession, only to have Anna counter with, "Or the profession's wrong." Anna's words stuck with me.

With each artifact I shared, it became clearer that, as teachers, we didn't feel like we had the power or control to define what it means to be a teacher. Our profession puts forth an image of an ideal teacher that we don't realize we've internalized until we're unable or unwilling to conform to it, at which point we become disappointed with ourselves as teachers and humans.

This was not the first time we talked about the impossible standards we place on ourselves as teachers, and our attempts to hide our humanness. Below is an excerpt from one of our early Group meetings when we were first getting to know each other around Audrey's table in April of 2013:

> Aubrey: Like how am I supposed to go to school and teach three-year-olds how to be the best people they can be when I'm doing ridiculous, not-healthy, not-safe, not-kind-to-myself things? I'm eating two-dozen cookies in two days, literally. How can I do that and then try to teach them how to be better people? That's something I very much struggle with. I am not good enough to teach them how to be good.
>
> Me: I think that being human in front of your students is a good thing, like being able to say, I made a mistake and I'm sorry. I've enjoyed being able to do that because it kind of brings you to a different level with them.

Hearing myself now, I want to give that earlier version of me a condescending pat on the back and smirk: "Just wait." But even as I mock my own naiveté, I still believe that showing my humanness to students is necessary. I just didn't know back then that it would involve me crying in front of them within my first semester of teaching.

The next fall, during my first full year of teaching, I also cried in front of my students. But it was somehow different. My own students reminded me of that moment at the end of the year, when I was sitting with them on the carpet, workshopping their persuasive essays. The assignment asked them to write a letter convincing their sixth-grade teachers to change a school policy. Abdillahi looked up from his paper and asked me, "Are the sixth-grade teachers mean or nice?"

I thought about how to answer this question, knowing Abdillahi and his anxiety around new experiences, but not knowing much about his future teachers. I responded, "They're probably like me: a little bit nice and a little bit mean."

Abdillahi seemed shocked, and exclaimed, "What?! You're *nice!*"

Sara, another student on the carpet, replied, "Yeah, you cried because we weren't listening to you at the beginning of the year."

My face turned red as I searched for what to say next, and stumbled upon something like, "can't you remember something else about me being nice?" I was embarrassed at first because, roughly eight months later, the students remembered the one day I most wanted them to forget.

"Line *up!*" I heard myself yelling. It was time for the students to go to gym, and I had lost control. Five boys wouldn't (or couldn't) keep their hands to themselves, which always led to a fight, which led to name calling, which led to me attempting to control the situation. It wasn't just that moment that led me to yell and eventually cry, it was the first few weeks of the school year culminating in this moment. Allen, a student with whom I had yet to form a connection, was the leader of this five-boy group that tore through the room in that moment as we were supposed to be lining up. I didn't cry because they wouldn't line up; I cried because my inability to line them up or stop them from being mean to each other reinforced all my suspicions that I was a shitty teacher and had no idea what I was doing. Not only did I not know what I was doing; the students, especially Allen, realized I had no control, and therefore continued their rampage around the room and into the hallway.

Just as I felt it was no longer possible to keep my tears at bay, I saw Mary, the math specialist, passing in the hallway. I grabbed her arm, and mouthed, "help me," as my red eyes and shaky voice betrayed me. Mary, a veteran teacher and all-around fantastic person, sprang into action, attempting to corral the students into a line. "Okay!" she said, "What are we trying to do here, Mrs. Mohan?"

I choked down my crying as best I could, and said to Mary, loud enough for students to hear: "We need to be in line to go to gym."

Noticing a difference in my voice, several students turned to look at me. "*She's crying!*" a student said, then another, and then another, until it traveled through the hallway to the other fifth-grade classroom next door. At that point, I was pretending to busy myself by the sink when a few of the other fifth-graders ran into the room to see if the rumor was true. "She *is* crying!"

A few moments later, a student from my class—I have no idea who it was—said, "Come on, this isn't a reality TV show." I will forever be grateful for that hilarious, well-intentioned student, even though their words didn't stop the gawking. Eventually, Mary took the students to gym, and I remained in the classroom, locked the door, and collapsed onto a beanbag chair so I could continue crying.

Fuck. Now I needed to stop crying so I could deal with the fact that the students saw me crying. Unfortunately, this wasn't the first time I'd cried in front of a class. The year before, during those six months of hell when I took over Victoria's classroom, I also cried in front of them. That time we'd had a healing circle with the school social worker.

I knew what I had to do now. The next morning we moved the kidney table, sat down on the floor, and had a healing circle. The students passed around the talking piece—a 10K finisher's medal I brought during the first week of school to represent something meaningful to me—and took turns answering the question, "Why do you think Mrs. Mohan was crying yesterday?" Most everyone, even Allen, said something along the lines of "we weren't listening to you." We discussed how weird it was to see someone cry who you normally don't: mom, dad, grandparent, teacher. Still totally mortified and worried I had screwed myself over for the rest of the year by showing weakness, I carried on with teaching, never to bring up the crying incident again.

But now, eight months later, Sara and Abdillahi were recalling that time I cried. I realized that they remembered this moment as an embodiment of my kindness—not weakness, or incompetence, but *kindness*. I'm positive the 2013 pre-teacher Amanda didn't expect to cry in front of her class in order to show her humanness, but an instance that was so raw and humiliating for me ended up connecting with the students in a way that I hadn't expected. My original rationale for the importance of appearing human was that it allows students to see their own humanness—something along the lines of, "Well, if my teacher is okay with making mistakes, then..." In all the reading I did in school, it was clear that students needed to feel comfortable, safe, in order to take risks in their learning; however, I also remember being horrified when I saw my parents as human for the first time: they *didn't* know all the answers? I eventually got over the initial shock, and understood them better as complete human beings, not just as my parents. Perhaps having a fifth-grade teacher prompt their discovery that we're all human will lead them to be more self-sufficient and accepting of others at an earlier age.

Or not.

Artifact 6: To Be Teacher

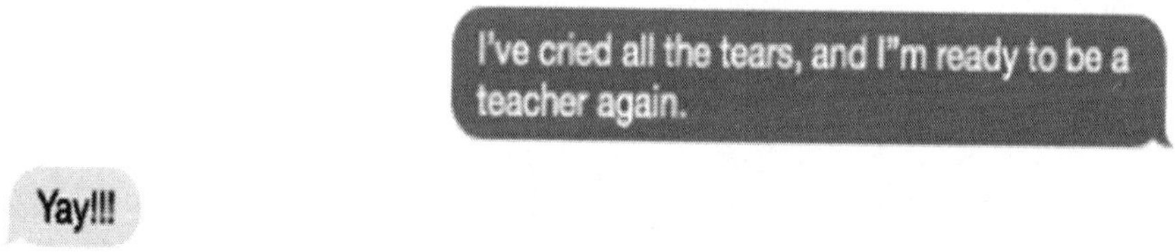

I've cried all the tears, and I"m ready to be a teacher again.

Yay!!!

Figure 7: To Be Teacher
Source: Author

When I sobbed on Jake's shoulder, not ready to go to bed because it meant waking up to be a teacher again, he would say, "you only have to go tomorrow." I both hated and loved this response. It's close to the "just for today" mantra of staying sober and I knew I could do that.

I would categorize my first six months of teaching just like that. Crying all the tears with nothing left to do but show up the next day and do it all again. A combination of sheer exhaustion and pure determination.

I kept fighting the fact that I'm a teacher. I had spent several days with my family, and discovered that my sister Meredith's job as a therapist was a lot like being a teacher. We both needed to show up for our "clients" in a perfect way. I've yet to develop my perfect way, but for her it consists of remaining neutral.

A colleague of mine observed that teaching is the only profession in which you see all your clients at once. Think about it: doctors, lawyers, real-estate agents, psychiatrists, psychologists all see their clients individually. I don't mean to imply that I can only teach one student at a time, but that, as a teacher, I feel unqualified to meet the needs of all students at all times.

Anna pointed out the disconnection I expressed between me as human and me as teacher. She said to me, "You keep saying, 'I'm ready *to be* teacher again' as if teacher isn't already part of you. It seems like you have to always make this choice like, 'now I'm going to *be* teacher.' For me it mirrors this idea of role playing: you are trying to change *into* a teacher instead of accepting the teacher and person you are."

I was fighting becoming a teacher even though it was my chosen profession. I was fighting it because the teacher I so badly wanted to be for my students couldn't exist in that fifth-grade classroom.

Figure 8: I'm Not Gonna Take Any Shit
Source: Author

Artifact 7

In artifact 7, the school day was better.

> **How did it go today?**
>
> **Better for me! Worse for the kids bc I was being a hardass**
>
> **Yeah! yeah! yeah!** 😭 😭 😭 😭 😭
>
> **I got a lot of "I hate you."**
>
> **But in teacher speak that's a good thing.**
>
> **It means they love you.**

Figure 9: Human/Teacher
Source: Author

Jake must have been relieved to hear that this day in the classroom was better. He saw me wailing the night before, unable to stop crying even to eat. I became the teacher I didn't want to be; a strict dictator. Colleagues told me that the kids needed it and there was no other way. I still don't know if that's the approach I will take on the first day of this school year.

I'm celebrating the fact that the school day was better, but only because I was a "hardass." My husband uses what I call the "I'm not gonna take any shit" lady emoji. I understand what he means by that, but I can't be that lady. I kind of want to be her—maybe it would ultimately be easier—but if I became her, then I'd no longer be who I am.

I've yet to figure out the formula for having a "good" day with the students. If a certain student or two is missing, then things might run smoothly, but there's really no rhyme or reason to the mood in the classroom. There's this never-ending need to appear positive, unchanging, unmoved, un-everything, while still maintaining care and compassion. I'm checking myself because sometimes I put expectations on myself and others that are completely made up and unrealistic, and I don't know I have them until I fail to meet them. But I don't think I'm making this one up. I've seen how my "humanness" can get in the way of my teaching this specific set of students. If I show any frustration or annoyance, it changes the mood of the entire classroom.

When I shared this writing with the Wild Horses at the cabin, the following conversation took place:

Me: I understand what he meant by that but I can't be like that.
Anna: What is like *that*?

Me: Like, "Nothing touches me!" In the moment, I got what he was saying. I kinda want to be this person, like maybe it would be easier if I was this person but if I was this person then I wouldn't be who I am.

Aubrey: Doesn't that go back even farther to an underlying institutional philosophy of what education should be? Whereas my personal philosophy might be to develop an empathetic community of global learners. I want children to grow up and be able to see other's pain and help each other out and care for each other, but institutionally, you need to read and answer the right questions. You need to do your math problems and get the right answer and graduate with a thing called a diploma and that's it. That's it.

I remember the hand motions I did when I said, "nothing touches me!" I looked a lot like the lady emoji with my forearms making an x across my body. During this conversation, the Wild Horses and I returned to the concept of teacher as human. Aubrey said she wants to teach students to grow up as empathetic, global learners, but how are we supposed to cultivate the humanness in our students when we feel like we need to hide our own humanness as teacher?

CONCLUSION

This is the part where I show you another text message I sent to Jake that exhibits me as a perfectly well-rounded, human teacher now that I've taken a close look at myself. Something like, "Good afternoon, darling! It was another great day of sharing and caring with my students. I'll be home early again to take Wally for a walk." Alas, no such artifact exists. However, I've come a long way since my panic attack in third grade and beginning treatment in Minnesota. I'd even say I've come a long way since my first six months as a teacher. Looking at artifacts, narrating and collectively (re)narrating with the Wild Horses allowed me to see connections between the work I did to get sober and my life now, as teacher. In spite of my own education, I was underprepared for how teaching would prey on my old insecurities. I'm not surprised anymore when the parts of me that are human show up in my classroom. I might even welcome them.

CHAPTER FOUR

We're All Learning

BY AUBREY HENDRY

This chapter begins with my experiences being observed, evaluated, and "mentored" as a first-year kindergarten teacher. I write about those and other stories from my first year of teaching, and then a little about my fear of evaluation. Then, I share three scripts I created, in the form of monologues, that have helped me reposition and (re)narrate difficult teaching days. Finally, I share an analysis the scripts in relation to the larger systems at play within schools.

ROUGH PATCH

I am the kind of person who likes to jump right in and share the big important news right away.

So that is how I will start.

My first classroom observation was unimaginable.

The second one was bad too.

In fact, it was a disaster. (But I am getting ahead of myself.)

I had finally been given the chance to have my own kindergarten classroom, and the first of three official evaluations was about to happen. I was nervous. My imagination nightmarishly swirled back to the two years before, when right after I received my teaching license I was hired for the year's final ten weeks after the previous teacher had been fired. Every step in that classroom was like walking through a battlefield. I remembered kindergarteners jumping on tables and bookcases and yelling at each other. I saw scissors fly across the room and trash from breakfast all over the floor. I saw the middle finger a lot; I saw rage. During those ten weeks, I counted the number of days when a chair was not thrown across the room in anger. I told the kids that if we got to five days with no chair throwing, then we could have a party. We never had that party.

I was told that safety was more of a priority than raising test scores. I counted down the days till the end. I worked hard, went to sleep at 6:00 p.m. and told myself it wasn't my fault.

Disasters

But when it came time for my first observation, in my first "real" classroom, I *never* saw myself failing. I never saw the red of "not proficient" on my evaluations. My worst-case classroom had already happened—I told myself that I had inherited that mess.

The lesson for my first observation had been planned holding hands with the person who promised to get me through the tenure process, my peer assistance reviewer (PAR). During the observation I felt confused, choppy, panicked, trying to remember a complicated sequence that was so unnatural. The second lesson was even worse. Even though so much of my teaching had improved, my evaluators saw a lesson I was unprepared for. It must have looked as though I had regressed (or somehow hidden how bad my teaching actually was).

On the day of that second *surprise* observation, I had planned to revisit rituals and routines in the morning. I planned that so my students could operate independently in the afternoon when I hoped I would be observed. I didn't expect them to show up when they did. I panicked. I tried to teach even though I did not have enough experience, used an easy "fall-back" lesson to simply teach, and I was not able to remain cool-headed. I hurried over to the math curriculum and looked at the lesson I had typed in my notes. Panic began to rise when I realized I hadn't finished planning that lesson. I had been so sure my evaluators wouldn't show the morning after a three-day weekend.

The previous week I had been waiting, holding my breath, looking toward the door, and hoping they saw each lesson. Thinking "this would be the one" because I had so many engaging things planned. Yes, *this lesson*. It had to be this one because I was using different ways of responding rather than raising hands. I was ready. Until, alas, a blessed three-day weekend. I had spent so much time planning other lessons that I forgot to go back and finish the morning ones. That was how I ended up with a score of "below standard" on the district's teacher-evaluation rubric, its standards of effective teaching (SET), again.

After those two evaluations, I grew to deeply dread and fear the next visit from a supervisor.

I knew that I was more than those evaluations. I grew. I learned. I asked for help. I heard feedback, assessed it, and put it to use in a way that was effective for me. My colleagues enjoyed working with me. My math and literacy coaches told me I was on the right track when I asked questions. I had been in the classroom in a variety of ways over the years and knew a lot about engaging students. My knowledge of songs and games exceeded most of my coworkers'. I had a large repertoire of cheers ("roller coaster," "fireworks," and "train," to name a few). I liked to take risks and make messes (like teaching students how frogs hibernate by painting over paper images of frogs with real mud). Yet somehow, the fear, anxiety, and the red on those evaluations, became me. The scores became how I felt and thought I looked in the classroom.

How could this be happening?

I'm Not Saying I was Amazing

In my memory, both of those lessons were far outliers, the worst examples of my teaching that explained the low average score. I'm not saying I was amazing. I'll be the first to admit that I have lot to learn. But between the first day of school and midwinter, in this lowest moment, I had learned so much about how to manage students, ask questions, and have a clear teaching point. These two lessons might seem so horrible because they are ingrained in my memory. I was evaluated with a twenty-four page SET rubric that has four possible rating categories: Below standard, developing, proficient, and exemplary. Most of my scores were in the red, falling into the below-standard category. With detailed observation notes and formal meetings to look at those red scores, how could any other lesson be worse—or more memorable?

The district conducted three formal observations for all pre-tenure teachers: Only one was announced, so you could plan a great lesson in advance. The next two were unannounced. You didn't have a window. Any time of day, any day of the week, and any lesson. You relied on your colleagues who had been observed to tell you that they (the principal and the PAR) had been in their room. That's how you knew you might be next.

Distrust

I didn't begin the year distrusting my PAR. But somehow, in our February meeting, I found myself looking at her and I realized a frozen panic sat inside of me. I had hoped to find support from her—after all, that was her job. However, after the first two observations, a few observational notes that didn't match my experience, and her lack of time spent supporting me, I found I couldn't rely on her. I worried constantly that she would judge me. I feared she would think things I never said. I interpreted her nonchalance and noncommittal reactions as her belief that I lacked skills. When she said our relationship was "like a triangle," that all the conversations we had together would be sent to the principal, and that any of her conversations with the principal would come back to me, it triggered something in me.

It was practically tattling to share everything with the principal!

I worried that my bluntness would get me into trouble, as it had during student teaching when I overshared my fears with my cooperating teacher and college supervisor. That's when I got called into a meeting at my college because they thought I was "unprofessional." Like Marie, I learned from my mom about how schools worked. Listening to my mom, who was also a teacher, I absorbed a distrust of authority. I overheard things like how building priorities and teacher expectations (like being in the building early rather than staying late) changed with each administrator. I understood that words could be used against you or misinterpreted.

No one is perfect, and if you want to get someone out of the field of teaching or out of your school, you can. Teaching is imperfect. Authority is arbitrary and subjective, even with rubrics. After my first two observations and because of my fear of surveillance, I chose to stay distant from my PAR.

Third Observation

I didn't cry at any point during that day or week because the third lesson that was observed wasn't awful. I know what awful is—I hang out with myself enough to know when things are going well and when they aren't. The third formal observation was average. Not amazing, but not horrible either.

I was told that the observations I had during my year of teaching kindergarteners were supposed to be "snapshots" that also took into account the whole. My employment by the district was not limited to those three observations. Or at least, that was my understanding. I understood that my growth—from that bottomless pit of horribleness, to where I ended the year—would matter. That growth was important. As teachers, we take growth into account when we look at student achievement. I thought the system would do the same for teachers in the early parts of their careers who are learning hand-in-hand with their students. This is not to say that teachers should slide through with no standards. I believe children deserve the best teachers. But it seemed like my PAR only saw my failures and no achievements.

I was recommended for nonrenewal. A fancy term for getting cut. After receiving this information and seeing the feedback from that observation I wrote. I wrote with fury. I want to share this with you, in the raw way it came out the first time.

April 23

I just got my last SET rubric back. On the section about using "self-reflection as a tool of growth" someone (either my PAR person—who is *supposed* to help me through tenure process—or principal) wrote, "The use of self-reflection is minimally evident. How might you reflect after each lesson to adjust and strengthen upcoming lessons?"

Do I reflect? I am furious. I believe I do. I have written reflections in my journal. I wake up in the middle of the night thinking about what went wrong and how to do it better next time. I take the little nugget of what works right as I'm doing it and store it in my head for later. I see things I don't like and think, "how and when am I going to reteach that skill?"

I despise the fact that, because I don't talk to you or send you my personal notes, you assume my self-reflection is minimal. Did you ever give me a floor to have a conversation with you after the second observation?

I disagree. I reflect but I don't reach the same decision or outcome that someone else would. That is where subjectivity comes in. Who says I don't reflect? SOMEONE WHO HAS NO RELATIONSHIP WITH ME!!! Did you ask my peers? My boyfriend? My sister? Did you call my mom? Did you read my journal or fucking watch me sleep and toss and turn as I came to realizations about what and why something went wrong?

NO.

NO!

WILD HORSES

During this year of teaching, the time I spent with the Wild Horses was like breathing. I didn't have to hold my breath, fearful that I would make a mistake. I could share what it felt like being watched. I could cry. Or laugh.

Minus the evaluations, I did feel like I was teaching. I was seeing a lot of growth in my students. This Writing Group, as I always called it even before we did lots of writing, was a place where my thinking could come out. We could laugh and cry together. My feelings could be shared about my insecurities, the successes, the absolute failures, the guilt of planning unsuccessful lessons, the fear of having a job, and the stress of completing coursework. Any or all was welcomed for discussion.

I have a lot to say and there are not often safe places with enough time or space that I get a chance to say the things that run through my mind. When we sat around Audrey's table and shared during our check-in time, there was space and time to just reflect and share. This place gave me a space to talk, where everyone understood how the papers pile up and the phone calls to parents need to be made, some way, somehow.

As we got to know each other, the ties and connections we shared about our mental well-being and the job became quite central to the discussions across the dark wooden table. Teaching practically preys on you if you are fearful. Fearful doesn't even describe it. Insecure, lacking confidence, unsure, about to burst into tears more than once a day walking down the hall. All of it is watched, noted, scored, and stored for later discussion in a meeting where there was never a "good enough" or "perfect." There can't ever be a feeling of completion.

This group helped me feel less alone, less stupid, and less stumbling. It became a place to hear that what I was doing or thinking was okay. Our group has helped me feel more thoughtful and caring.

In a meeting at work, you're focused on the goals, the data, and picking up students from their specialist and trying to go to the bathroom in between. After school, colleagues have families to go home to and take care of, other jobs to go to, or errands to run. At home, the partner doesn't always totally get it or feels so much frustration it is almost counterproductive to share. So there, around the table, we finally had the space to share the things we'd been struggling with, the sad stories, and the hilarious stories.

They understood how badly I wanted to be a "proficient" teacher in that first year. When I spoke, the sets of eyes at the table didn't glaze over after ten straight minutes of talking about a mini-lesson. It was understood that each question you ask must be phrased *just the right way* to elicit just the right answer from the specific group of kids. And then the question must be followed up by a more difficult question for the students who thought the first question was too easy. It was known that *the order* in which you say things matters entirely; you can't say "line up in order of tallest to shortest"—you must say "when I say *go*, you will put yourself in order from tallest to shortest. The tallest person in the front, the shortest person in the back." One simple misdirection can lead to chaos and crying. I was heard and absolutely empathized with at our writing table, when I shared things like the time a child got so mad at me redirecting him that he whipped the dramatic play sink across the center and broke it.

These anecdotes might be criticized and critiqued in other settings. But in our group, the idea that what I was sharing might have made me seem incompetent never crossed my mind. I felt that no matter what I said, the women in our group understood I wasn't a bad teacher. I was trying my best to do what I thought was right. You really are trying your best, even though you do not know what these little humans will do.

We, as a collective, get it.

How a Simple Snapshot Inspired Me

Until that first year of teaching, I don't think I completely understood all of pressures we as teachers face. Our little group was a place to gain back some strength and wholeness.

During our summer writer's workshop (which took place before all of the negative evaluations I have described above), Anna asked us to write from the perspective of a person in a photo that we'd selected as an artifact. I found a photo of a child lying in the book nook of a classroom when I was a pre-K arts and science specialist (the year between the ten weeks I talked about before and the awful year of being "non-renewed"). My job was to create and implement daily fifty-minute lessons for pre-K students in two different classrooms. I was alone in classrooms while the teacher had her prep time. I know I was struggling to control the children. Looking at the photo allowed me time to consider several four-year-old students who had presented themselves often as defiant or noncompliant. I wrote to try to figure out a way to access their voice and get into their heads.

In the workshop, I wrote a series of monologues sparked by the question, "What are students thinking?" No, that's not right. The question was more like a hair-pulling shriek: "*What are you thinking??????*" I thought that if only I could get into their heads, I could meet them where they were at.

The scripts that I wrote and share below run along a risky line of danger. I am a white woman and the students whose voices I wanted to access in my writing are black. There is a long, negative history of white people using African American English for humor or to misrepresent a group of people; that is not what I sought to do here. But I felt that to leave out my student's racial identity was to do them an injustice, whitewashing them, painting them as not worthy of being themselves, and using a colorblind viewpoint. However, by keeping their language in place, I risked creating a picture that includes stereotypes and assumptions that were based in my whiteness. That was not my intention. My portrayals were grounded in conversations and interactions with these students.

Script 1

The main character in the first monologue is Prince, a fictitious four-year-old child. In this script, I based each event on my observations of his behaviors that made me, as teacher, feel out of control.

From the Perspective of Prince, age four

Setting: A school.

Enter Prince. (Smiling)

Prince: Hey. I see somebody I know! I better go say hi to them and see what they're doin'.

(Runs out the 'no' door. Adult reacts unfavorably.) (Frowning) They don't like me anymore.

Maybe they'll wanna play with me. If I run away we can play tag. (Begins running.) This is fun. They makin' a real funny face at me. Why can't we do this all the time? (Adult voice speaks) Wha—Take a break? I'm outta here. (Runs back into the classroom then slows. Notices other children.) Wait a minute. (Slowly says) People are playing without me. That teacher don't like me. I don't like her either. I don't like when kids play without me. (Runs again and knocks down blocks creating a loop in the classroom.) It's funny when they cryin'. They don't like playin' with me. I wonder if Teacher still likes me. She probably don't either. (Jumps on sensory table, smiling, arms up in the air.) This is so fun. I feel so big! School's fun like this! (Teacher directs Prince to get down.) (Loudly) Fuck you bitch.

(Re)narrating

As you can "hear," I struggled to get Prince to do what I wanted him to do. He had his agenda and I had mine. As a travelling teacher, I would arrive each day after lunch with my squeaky, roll-y cart with tubs of toys or musical instruments. I was ready to go. But Prince had other ideas. By creating a script that highlighted my difficult interactions with Prince and many other children in those classrooms, I was able to reconsider the question: Who has the power?

In classrooms where the teacher struggles with "management," the children are in control—or rather, out of control. However, when you look into classrooms that are managed well, it is the children who are in control. They are empowered and seem to run the classroom with a self-directed assuredness. All of us have our own agendas. Children have their own agendas just as much as the teacher who wants to meet standards, benchmarks, and hit team goals. And yet, we have so little control over what is going on in a child's brain. This script allowed me to think and wonder: Whose agenda is more important? Mine as teacher? Or theirs—as student, child, and learner? What were the relationships between agendas and power?

Script 2

I also had questions about another four-year-old student I call Rontay. Rontay was puzzling. In certain spaces, he adhered to the rules very closely. In other spaces, just moments apart, his body seemed completely out of control. I wondered how much the relationships he had with teachers in particular spaces impacted his behavior. I wrote this monologue and could hear his smart, clear voice in my head, teaching about how to be at school.

From the Perspective of Rontay, age four

Setting: A school bus.

Enter Rontay (smiling)

Rontay: Every morning when I wake up, I gotta go to school. Sometimes we get to have breakfast and sometimes we don't. I gotta ride the bus sometimes. And you always be no hittin', no kickin', no pushin', no runnin', and no takin' stuff from other kids. You sit on your seat and you wait 'til you get to school. It's hard. (Looks up, hears female bus driver voice saying) Rontay! No punching! And no running! Sit down now or we're going to have to call your mom again! (Laughing) She don't really know my mom she's just sayin' that. People always actin' like they know my mom, but they don't. Just my teacher. She and my mom always be talkin'.

Setting: School cafeteria.

Enter Rontay (smiling)

Rontay: (Serious tone) When you get to school, you go get your breakfast. You gotta wait your turn. And then you get cereal or yogurt or apples or oranges or bananas or waffles or eggs and milk and juice and crackers! (Looks up, hears lunch lady in his head) Rontay! No budging! You have to wait for your turn! Why she always be talkin' to me? I gotta get to class to see my teacher! (Moves from cafeteria to hallway) (Looks over, hears male teacher voice) Rontay! No running! Go back and walk!! (Frowning, eyes lower) I can't go back and walk, my teacher needs her hug!! (Told to go into classroom.) (Turns to audience, finger wagging) You always use your walking feet. Then, you hug your teachers really tight (arms out in imaginary hug) 'cuz they like that and then, you put your backpack away and then, you write your name. If you write your name real nice, your teacher likes it. (Smiles)

Setting: Classroom

Enter Rontay (spots adult teacher on the side, smiles, we hear a female voice) Rontay! Look at your name! You wrote all the letters all by yourself! That's so great! You're having a writing morning! Come give me a hi-five! (Smiles, turns to audience) See? When you sit and eat your breakfast you have to be responsible, be respectful, and be safe. And keep your hands to yourself. We get reminders. Rontay! We use kind hands in this classroom. If she says 'stop,' you need to stop!! Take a break until you're ready to be respectful! Next time I gotta tell her I will help open her milk. Friends like when you tell them what you're thinking. (Smiles big) I'm ready to come back now.

(Re)Narrating

My scripts were based on what I imagined Prince and Rontay were thinking. They became new artifacts and with them, I was able to think about motivations. What was the motivation for running down the hall? What was the purpose of doing your "job," as we so often ask our young learners to do?

I realized that for Rontay, it was all about the relationship. The relationship motivated it all. During this monologue, there are adults who play opposite roles. The first is the bus driver, the cafeteria lady, and the hallway monitor, who like commanders said, "Do this, stop that, no this, no that!" The different role that teacher played was more of a guide. The commanders saw only the negative about what Rontay did. There was no awareness that Rontay ran down the hall to see the teacher, only knowledge that he was not following the rules, again. The adults shouted that he needed to go back or wait and only a sense of exasperation with the belief that *that is Rontay*. The adult as commander used language to tell Rontay what he can't do. Once Rontay got to the classroom—with the teacher as guide, who was supportive and proud—he said "good morning" respectfully and did his job writing his name without reminders. Rontay was motivated by the relationship with this teacher to perform tasks and be kind to others. When Rontay didn't follow the rules, there were reminders, redirection for next time, and a consequence which he chose to complete.

By writing these scripts, I took up a different perspective. The writing allowed me to become an "observer" with both creative license and hard evidence. Repositioning myself gave me the ability to analyze the scenario as though it was a case study. I could imagine the motivations of four-year-olds. I could allow both the humor and possible answers to come through. In the moment, that was not always possible.

Even though these monologues were all just in my head, the (re)narration of various scenarios gave me back some power. I could take a step back and have a laugh at the ridiculousness of me as teacher trying to gain "control" over a four-year-old who just wants to say "hi." I could believe that children forget rules because they were motivated by greater things, like love for a teacher. I recognized too that my identity as a white female teacher, who taught children of color, continued to affect my worries about control and teaching.

But the monologues, first in my head and now on paper, became powerful to me. I wondered: Could this kind of writing—writing and analyzing scripts—help me learn to reposition and (re)narrate my awful experiences being evaluated as a first-year teacher? Could I gain back some of the power that my evaluations seemed to have taken from me? Could this in turn somehow be used with students so they too could gain control?

NEW GROUND

After writing the scripts for Prince and Rontay, and having the time and space to re-narrate my understanding of a compiled set of moments with them, I realized that I had a running script in my head that my evaluators couldn't see. My self-talk, my inner monologue didn't appear to observers as I was being watched. I began to wonder: What was I, as teacher, thinking as I taught? What were my observers missing? There was a discrepancy between what they were seeing from my performance and what I was thinking in my head. Like the children in my scripts who had motivations and thoughts running through their heads, I did too. I had a lot of teaching knowledge, yet they said the evidence of my knowledge of pedagogy was lacking. How could that be?

I wrote a monologue of my inner thoughts in the same way I did with my four-year-old students. I thought that if I could get into my head, I could see where I went wrong or what I was actually doing right. The writing of the scripts allowed me to (re)narrate the experience of my observation. In what follows, I have provided portions of the official lesson plan for the observation accompanied by, in parenthesis, my thoughts during the third observation during my first year of teaching.

The Lesson Plan and My Thinking

Setting: My kindergarten classroom, 20 five-year-olds, sitting criss-cross applesauce on the carpet. It is April 18, 2016. Math instructional time for Math Unit 4.21.
Enter: Evaluators with laptops.
Me: (This is it. Smile.) Objective: I can name and describe 3D shapes. (Thank god I stated the objective. That's what they want, a clear teaching point and restating of the objective several points throughout.) (Now to pre-assess. Lift up learned shapes.) Raise your hand. What shape is this? (Hold up one: sphere then cube) (By asking students what they know already, I am differentiating; it lets me know what to teach, what to go deeper in and how much review we need. They told me in training that pre-assessing what students know is a way to differentiate. Raising their hands is a surefire way to show clear behavior expectations, which they said I needed to work on in February. Yes!) Clap two times if you agree. (Kids do not all respond that way) (Okay that didn't work, it must have been because I wasn't giving clear directions. Shit, shit, shit, I need to do better. Don't panic. Slow down.) Who can raise their hand and describe what's special about this shape? (Okay, that worked better this time.) We had cones on a table during morning work time. (Nod head) (I am connecting to prior knowledge—that is a part of the SET. And I referred to the objective again. Good job, you can do this. Slow down.) That was an experience they had this morning and all of them touched and experimented with the cones. That's connecting to prior knowledge.) Everyone say cone: say it, cone, clap it cone, tap it, cone. It's one syllable. (Holding it is for visual learners only, but they all got to feel the word by tapping. I know that I am not passing it around for kinesthetic learners but my math coach suggested I don't because they have already had time holding it many other times, it has been in the math center for an entire week.) Time to share. Who would like to share what is like a cone? (Allowing their connections to be heard and shared. I'm going to use pick sticks because I don't really like "raise your hand") (Continue with curriculum questions) What shape is on the bottom of the cone? Is it 2D or 3D? (The questions in the curriculum are getting "harder"—isn't that scaffolding learning????) (Oh gosh they are getting wiggly) (I whisper to my neighbor student) You need to sit on your pockets or I can't sit by you. (That must have looked pretty good because he fixed it after redirection and not getting called out that was good, right?) Ok. Let's all stick our legs out straight. Wiggle them. (I'm going with the flow, I'm not sticking to my lesson only, that's something they told me to do. Thank goodness. I'm doing it. It's not horrible.) (Time for closure) Today we did something very important, we named and talked about what makes each 3D shape special. (Hell yeah, I even got the closure in!!!) (Transition: Send kids to have to's.) Time for have-tos. Nicely done. (Okay I'm reviewing expectations. Clear expectations—that's good. Kids are on task. I'm holding my breath. They are doing differentiated learning, that is based on data. Differentiation is huge on the SET. I'm helping my students who need more time naming their shapes.) (Notices evaluators) (Frowns) (Wait, why aren't they leaving? Why the fuck aren't they leaving? She's following me around with her computer. She's typing.) (Okay. I need to do my 3D shape assessment for the PLC (Professional Learning Community)

this week. I am not doing groups today because it's Monday, my particular group of students has shown they need more adult support on Monday, I am reconnecting and building relationships. They will see that.) (Fuck, she's in the reading center looking at the books. That's the one thing that I know isn't done. That's not good. I just went through them but didn't organize them properly. She's disgusted or disappointed, she sees it's lacking. I know it's lacking, that's something that I couldn't tackle this year. There were too many books. At least there are areas of study and they get switched monthly.) (Holy shit, they finally left.) (Teaching assistant TA reached out his hand: "Hi-five, Ms. Hendry, we did good.") Yes! We did! (And I'm not crying.)

(Re)narrating

Writing about this moment gave me the power to (re)narrate my observer's proclamation of "not-proficient." Writing the script let me relive the moment. I saw my hyper-awareness of the standards to which I was being held. I was aware of the rubric and really thought I was on track. Yes I did that, no I didn't do that, proficient, failure. I was screaming encouragement to myself to keep going because "I can do it" while simultaneously losing confidence as I watched my evaluator's blah face reveal nothing about how she was "objectively" rating my performance. It breaks my heart to know that a simple lesson about cones ripped me to shreds on the inside. I just wanted to be a good teacher. Each time I stumbled or did something "wrong," it impacted my perception of the lesson. After (re)narrating and analyzing my first kindergarten classroom experience, I realized I needed three significant things, that I will explain below, to feel supported and successful. They are: (1) trust and truth in relationships; (2) belief in…; and (3) we're all learning.

Trust and Truth in Relationships

Through my rewriting of the lesson, it was clear to me that I did not trust the PAR evaluator. If I'd had a more trusting relationship, I might have felt comfortable having a dialogue with her about my teaching. Like Prince and Rontay, the thoughts in my head were and are valid, regardless of what showed on the outside.

Let's compare some of the systems at play in each of the scripts. For simplicity's sake I am going to say that there are three systems: students, teachers, and administrators. Within Prince and Rontay's scripts, the teacher–student relationship was the focus. In the lesson-plan script, the administrator–teacher relationship was the focus. Each script contained one individual that had power and one individual that needed support. Both pairs of relationships should have a learner and a mentor. I believe that administrative relationships with teachers should be supportive and have an aspect of trust, just as we believe teacher relationships should be supportive of students.

Within a teacher–student relationship, the teacher is hired to teach, guide, support, and move their students from wherever they are to wherever they need to be. From my experience, one way to do this is to step aside and view the child as a case study. This new angle allowed me to recognize the needs and desires of my students. As Prince stood on top of the sensory table, I could sense his feeling of power. I knew it was very important that I didn't simply observe him, but also that I spent time interacting with him to build a mutual trust. I took time to talk and ask questions of him as we built castles together in the block center, knowing that I would make no progress without a trusting relationship. After learning his interests, I sought out toys that would engage him. With Rontay, relationships were central to his success in the school setting. He had success with the teachers with whom he had strong relationships. The bus driver and the cooks in the lunchroom would say that they knew his mom, but he knew enough to know that they didn't. His *real* teacher knew his mom. The teachers in the hall knew his name and behaviors but didn't know how to make those behaviors meaningful for him. His *real* teacher had a meaningful relationship with him that supported his ability to follow classroom expectations.

I have attempted to distance myself from the artifact (script) I created of my teaching and my inner thinking. I decided to call myself "teacher" instead of using me/I. In this scenario, the administrator watched the teacher. The teacher saw only the administrator typing each phrase that came out of the teacher's mouth and counting the number of students who responded to various questions. The teacher understood that the administrator believed she was typing pure objective commentary and notes about events. Did the administrator believe the teacher is doing her best? Did the teacher trust the administrator? This internal monologue sounded scared and fearful, rather than confident. Unlike a teacher-student relationship, this was not a reciprocal learning relationship.

Clearly, I believed and expected that the relationship with my supervisors would go beyond them evaluating me. As I worked with children who made me question and adjust my practice, I took time to watch them and often approached my students as an observer; at other times, I needed to build a trusting relationship with them so that my new knowledge could be effective in working with them. Different than a daily or friendly check-in, my evaluators showed up unannounced with computers and Excel-formatted documents. That's what it was called, an "unannounced observation." It felt like they were trying to catch me in a bad light.

Belief in…

As teacher, we are always striving to dig deeper, know our students more, and push them farther. As teacher, I had a choice to view Prince through his behavior only or to view his behavior as having deeper meanings. If I chose to think, "Oh, Prince can't follow the rules," then I would have given up on him and he would have felt that. I chose to continue to question myself and work to ensure his success. I chose to believe in him.

Looking at Rontay's script as an artifact, I noticed that there was a difference used by Rontay's classroom teacher and other staff at school. His teacher used language that showed a belief in his capacity to follow expectations: "Be respectful" or "Tell her I need help." Just like Rontay, my inner monologue changed based on my understanding of how I was being evaluated.

In my teacher education program, I was taught about a deficit view and self-fulfilling prophecies and how negatively those impact students. I understood a deficit view to be the belief that students lack the needed skills (academic, social) to achieve academic success. I understood that if I had a deficit view of students, they would meet those expectations. As a teacher I learned (and I agree) that this deficit view was unacceptable. Ironically, it seemed to be the main way my supervisor interacted with me.

The language on the SET became the reflection of the beliefs I thought my evaluators had of me. Because I was being marked below standard, I came to believe that that was all I was capable of. I had no indication that my evaluator believed in my capacity to perform well. I wish my evaluator had chosen to believe in me.

We're All Learning

Teachers do not learn it all in their first year of teaching. Teaching is hard. It is frustrating. It is aggravating. Its variables are ever-changing. What worked today might not work tomorrow. What worked tomorrow might fail in three weeks. It's like juggling a hundred tasks and *then* adding the students and their unique needs. They all have to be spun at specific heights and speeds. During my first year, I was not able to spin them all. I wasn't able to meet each of my students' needs.

I, as teacher, am also a learner. I reached out to my students with the knowledge that they are filled with experiences to draw on. My evaluators did not do the same for me. All of the research done on best practices for children can also be applied to adults. We are all people, learning. It is hypocritical to state that I, as teacher, must view students with a growth mindset, but my administrators can critique my learning with a deficit view. The public school system needs to retain teachers. But it seems like there is an "out to get you" and a "sink or swim" attitude toward teachers. Just as teachers with students, our priorities for teachers, all teachers, should be to offer support, mentorship, and feedback based within a shared relationship, because that is what learners need.

Some major issues in the current structure of teaching and learning to teach include: Teacher evaluation, subjectivity within those evaluations, pressures on new teachers to close the achievement gap, the fact that teachers have a limited apprenticeship before being completely in charge, new teachers teaching high-needs students when they themselves are also learners, white female teachers still being the most prevalent group entering teaching, high teacher burnout, and lack of teacher retention. Despite all of these systemic issues, students still need to learn and teachers still need to (learn to) teach their students. After each failure of an observation, and with no relationship or support from my evaluator, I deeply considered leaving the field of teaching. Though I saw large amounts of growth in my students, that wasn't enough to balance out the lack of encouragement and support with all of the personal and heartbreaking aspects of teaching.

Conclusion

I keep thinking about how my experience as a first-year teacher felt like being thrown off a cliff. I wasn't sure I would make it, even with previous years of experience in classrooms. Should that be? Should it be that hard? If only my principal had looked beneath or beyond the observation notes she received about those three lessons, maybe I wouldn't have been "recommended for non-renewal."

Soon after the devastating experience of being "nonrenewed," I interviewed for a kindergarten position in a new district I prepared and taught a lesson with several people observing and evaluating me. As you can imagine, I was terrified but also determined. The outcome of the interview, positive or negative, would affirm or undermine my prior evaluations and eventual nonrenewal. I was shocked by the positive comments that I heard from the principal who observed me teach a lesson for twenty six of their kindergarten students. It was the most positive feedback I'd had all year.

I was hired on the spot.

CHAPTER FIVE

Teacher as a Role to Play

BY MARIE D.S. VOREIS

LEARNING TO PLAY SCHOOL

School is essentially the family business. My mom is a high school English teacher. My aunt was a children's librarian. My uncle is a school social worker. My grandpa was a high school band director. Both grandmas. My cousin and her husband. My great aunt and uncle.

My grandma Harriet was particularly proud of my choice to go into education. Shortly after I got my license, she sent her first teaching contract home with my dad. It is framed on my desk in my office. Harriet Ruth Hladky was hired to teach fourth grade in 1945 for a salary of $1,350. We never exchanged many stories about being teachers, but I sensed a shift in our relationship after I got my license, as if we were connected by an unspoken code used among those who have stood in front of a classroom and appeared to have some authority.

I'm sure my grandma Mary would have been proud too, but she died before I was born. We shared a middle name and an eye color, the only blue eyes in the family. My mom laments our inability to meet for many reasons, but especially because grandma was a teacher too.

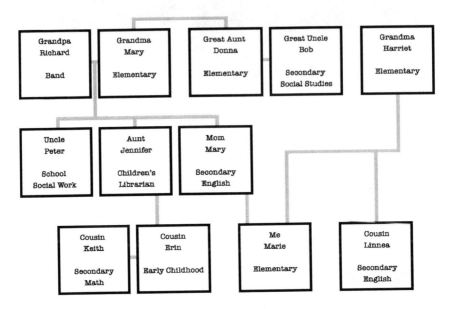

Figure 1: Teaching: A Family Tradition
Source: Author

My best friends, when I was two and three years old, were my mom's colleagues and my "English teacher moms," which led me to form sentences such as, "My mother and I often have frozen yogurt as a snack after school." I insisted on knowing the author and illustrator of every book I read. When I got a little older, I spent hours at school during teacher prep week, playing doctor in empty classrooms with other teacher's kids, hanging posters on the cork boards, and writing messages on the chalkboard for her students to find on the first day of school.

Figure 2: Playing in the School Cafeteria Line with My Mom, 1988
Source: Author

One of my favorite tasks during teacher prep week was moving books from the book room to my mom's classroom. She would make me a list of what she needed and send me with her keys and an empty metal cart down the long hallway, across the window-lined skyway, around the corner to the book room door. It looked like a closet because it was. A generic school plaque outside the door stated only a room number. I loved feeling like I was in on a secret of the school. High schoolers walked by this door every day and didn't know what lay on the other side. I made a ceremony of inserting the key into the lock, turning the handle, and entering the tiny closet filled with a labyrinth of shelves and multiple copies of textbooks and novels.

I always took a lap around the room before I consulted the list my mom had made for me. I ran my hand over the spines lined up on the shelves, reading the titles aloud as I went. *The Adventures of Huckleberry Finn, Romeo and Juliet, To Kill a Mockingbird, Elements of Literature,* and *Vocabulary for the High School Student.* My type-A, ever-organized little brain loved the patterns created by the book spines, the way they were uniform, and grouped according to title and size. There were usually boxes of books waiting to be shelved piled on the floor around the room, and sometimes, I would take extra time to add the boxed books to the shelves if I could find space for them.

Eventually, I would get around to the list my mom had made and start taking books from the shelves to my cart. I would challenge myself to see how many books I could lift from the shelf at one time, holding onto just the two on either end, and move to the cart without dropping them. By the time I was finished, I couldn't see over the cart anymore so I made the long trek back to the classroom, looking around the end of cart, and bumping into walls several times during the journey.

I came to school to help, and I learned how to play school. Not in the way I often "played school" at home, teaching my mom or little sister the alphabet with flashcards or giving them homework to finish. Teacher was a character, and I learned to play the role. I learned how much work and planning goes into setting up a classroom for the beginning of the year. I learned how deeply my mom was affected by the comments of parents and administrators. I learned how deeply she cared about each one of her students. I learned how teachers talk to each other, but perhaps more importantly, about one another. I learned how many hours teachers spend grading at the dining room table every night.

While my friends did chores around their houses like vacuuming, putting away the dishes, and making their beds, I spent hours sitting at the dining room table helping my mom grade papers. From the time I was in eighth grade, I sat at the head of the table and she on the side. We started a Disney movie on the TV to provide background noise. The movie choice never mattered (though we loved *Aristocats* and later, *Harry Potter*). Once, my mom put *The Emperor's New Groove* on and the menu played on loop for at least half an hour before anyone noticed. The stack of papers, sometimes as many as 100, sat between us, slowly, slowly, slowly getting smaller. I would pull a paper in front of me along with the carefully crafted rubric and my pen color of choice.

Different colored pens were one of the many coping mechanisms my mom had developed over time. "Keep mixing it up! What color do you want now?" I usually started with orange or magenta and set to work checking for comma splices and misformatted works-cited pages. I graded vocabulary quizzes and counted journal entries. If research papers were involved, I counted sections and paragraphs within sections. Does the works-cited match the parenthetical documentation? Does every section include multiple sources? I recorded missing items on the rubric before passing the paper over to my mom to read for content. It was like our own assembly line of assessment. Checking off requirements and hoping the stack would get smaller faster. I tried to sit up straight but the "hunch" would inevitably win. As if a magnetic field sloped my shoulders toward the papers, the muscles in my shoulders and neck were so tight I had to force them back to an upright position. I coped with the pain by making the piles of finished papers neater and finding a new pen.

When I was in high school, my best friend joined the production. Matt was a fairly permanent fixture in my house during those years, so he became part of the family. He made himself at home in front of the TV and joined in my required tasks. He even had to help me weed the rocks lining my parents' driveway, after we made one particularly ill-advised decision for which we were caught, and weeding rocks was deemed the appropriate punishment.

One day after we got home from play rehearsal, my mom was grading papers at her usual dining room spot. Matt eagerly offered to help, mostly because he liked to read the students' writing to feel better about his own writing skills. I agreed to join in simply because I had nothing better to do. We positioned ourselves around the table, grabbed our chosen pen colors—mine was orange, his red—and started in on the stack of college essays. We chatted and read aloud examples of good and poor writing. Eventually, my mom left us with the stack of papers to go make dinner, and in her absence, Matt found a paper that needed a lot of work. He wrote, in his chosen red pen, a giant "F" in the upper corner of the paper, and then proceeded to staple the bottom corner of the paper together so the pages could no longer be separated. He wasn't invited back to our assessment assembly line for quite some time after my mom discovered the paper, cut off the corner with the giant "F," removed the staple, and made an apologetic excuse to the student about spilling sticky jam on the paper that couldn't be wiped off.

I always found grading to be an enjoyable chore. I would much rather help grade vocabulary quizzes than do the laundry or dishes. It was work, but it was social. There was something about grading papers that was deeply rooted in playing school. The fact that assessment and feedback are part of the job is clear even to people who have only experienced school from a student's perspective. Of course, for nonteachers and my high school self, grading was a fun, "teacher-y" task. Marking a quiz question right or wrong. Giving a score based on a list of requirements. Grading felt powerful.

Now that I have my own students' work to grade, the power is gone. Now it is mundane and disconnected from the learning that happens inside the classroom. I want to give feedback that helps students grow academically and seek new information, but time determines the type of feedback I give. Marking an assignment on a one-to-four scale is much faster than writing commentary. Now the pile in the middle of our dining room table has become two: my mom's and mine, college essays and elementary literary analyses, research papers and geometry, journal entries and arithmetic. And when we can't get to the same table, the piles are separated by a few miles and a phone call. The different-colored pens still serve to make the work a little more enjoyable. Now my husband and sister-in-law have adopted my role of playing teacher and helping me grade, and they feel powerful.

I spent so much time in and around schools growing up that walking into a school feels like coming home. The mildew smell of books passed through years of student hands. The scuffed tile floors and generic carpet. The chalkboards that have been covered by whiteboards that have been covered by SMART Boards. The shelves that strain under the weight of materials, and tables covered with the marks students have left behind. These things somehow exist no matter if the school I enter is familiar or new. But in these buildings, I knew who I was and how I was expected to be. I knew what a "teacher" looked like and how to embody that role.

I knew how to play school.

I knew enough how to play the kind of teacher that administrators wanted walking through their hallways and teaching in their classrooms. I knew enough to become the teacher who appeared to have it all together. I fit the typical teacher stereotype. I am a white, middle-class, heterosexual woman. I am married. I hope to have a few children. I am the type of person who others assume isn't struggling, but I am also the person who panics every Sunday night (and sometimes Monday and Tuesday, too).

Panic Backstage

Love and panic aren't emotions that intersected in other areas of my life, but every Sunday morning I woke up with a tiny, anxious boulder in the pit of my stomach. While I leisurely drank my cup of coffee and took the dog for a morning walk, the boulder was easy to ignore. As the day went on, I was increasingly convinced that Monday morning would bring disaster. I wouldn't be ready for my lessons. I'd forget about the form I was supposed to deliver to the social worker. I'd oversleep my alarm and wake up after school had already started. I'd fooled everyone into thinking I knew what I was doing so far, but tomorrow, they'd find out I actually had no idea. With every self-doubting thought, the tiny boulder grew until, by dinner time, it had grown to fill my stomach with a clenching, heavy dread.

Before I started teaching, I spent three years as a professional stage manager. I watched countless rehearsals where actors crafted their roles. I made sure performances went off without disaster, under perfect lighting, and well-timed sound cues. And I watched as actors left their carefully created characters on the stage, leaving their performances for the next show. So, when I started teaching, I had a sense of the role I was playing as teacher. I was well versed in the characters of schools, having observed a wide variety of teachers in my childhood. I pieced together the best parts of all of them to craft my role and felt ready to step onto my classroom stage.

But even with all of that preparation, I continued to fall apart in a storm of stress. This particular tendency to fall apart occurred in everything I did, teaching and otherwise. When I had a deadline for a paper coming up, I worried, stressed, cried, swore, and came up with a great product. I knew how to craft what teachers are looking for. When I had a busy weekend full of fun things with no time for my introverted self to unwind, I worried, stressed, cried, swore, and had a great time. When I had an observation at school coming up I worried, stressed, cried, swore, and got great scores. I knew how to act the part when someone was watching me teach. Apparently, worry, stress, crying, and swearing were necessary before I could feel successful. What the hell was that about? I'd learned that in order to perform as teacher, I had to fall apart before the spotlight was on me so no one would see the cracks in my act.

One colleague said that Friday at 2:05 p.m., right after the buses had been waved away to carry the students home for the weekend, was the best moment of her week. Every minute after that only brought us closer to Sunday and the crushing inevitability of Monday. My anxiety fed on the regularity of Monday morning and had me thoroughly convinced that disaster was impending, waiting to show my weaknesses and reveal my incompetency. I managed to hide my anxiety behind my performance as teacher, but only until the next Sunday.

WILD HORSES

When Karen invited me to the group Audrey was starting, I was excited to have a place to examine becoming a teacher in a nonacademic setting. I felt like my teacher-licensure classes weren't telling the whole story because, being a teacher's kid, I knew about the long hours and the phone calls and emails to concerned parents. I knew about the politics of schools. I was learning the pedagogy and the content but the setting was too sterile. Maybe because of all of the playing school of my childhood, I knew that I wasn't getting the whole story about what being teacher really meant. We weren't talking about the fears that were surfacing as I got closer to having my own classroom. We weren't talking about how to support a classroom full of students who were functioning across four or five or six grade levels of understanding. Differentiation was more of a buzzword than a practiced skill. I knew my pretty lesson plans, aimed at pleasing my professors and getting top scores, were not the key to my success or sanity. I had no idea how essential our group would become to me. They helped me understand how my role as teacher intersected with being human.

It was often hard to get myself to our writing sessions. Between working full time and finishing my teaching license, I was mentally and physically exhausted. The twenty-minute drive to Audrey's felt like work. There were so many other things I should have been doing: writing papers, writing lesson plans, doing laundry, and going grocery shopping. I had every excuse.

I also knew that as soon as I was settled around Audrey's dining room table again, I would find comfort that didn't exist anywhere else, because my teacher-self needed other teachers who were on the same journey; who experienced minute-to-minute, hour-to-hour, day-to-day victories and failures in a classroom; who felt exhausted, overwhelmed, exhilarated, and determined; who questioned their decisions to choose teaching as a profession; who understood the subtext of my stories.

At one of our meetings, Aubrey expressed her frustration at the public's perception of what teachers do all day. People heard kindergarten and they thought: tying shoes, playing in the sand, finger painting, "Pinterest and polka dots." They don't realize that kindergarten was actually all of those things plus teaching how-to writing and poetry to children who didn't yet know how to form a sentence. In my classroom, fourth and fifth grade was covering how to manage your emotions as your body prepared for the raging hormones of preadolescence and counseling social problem-solving skills while also teaching how to calculate the area of irregular shapes. My teaching was also watching for signs of unrest or distress in each child, creating a culture of safety, routine and kindness, preempting behavior problems brewing across the classroom, and dispelling parent fears and concerns, all while delivering academic content. At any given moment, my mind was in six different places at once, trying to juggle so many needs. So it was invaluable to have a group of people who knew all the layers happening under the surface story I had to share. I needed our group as therapy, comfort, and reassurance.

And so I came, sat in a dining room chair and shared my story: ups, downs, triumphs, doubts, uncertainties, and big life decisions. These women were there when I started dating my now-husband. They were there when I started my long-call sub jobs and when I was offered the Montessori position. They were there when I had to decide if I was going back to grad school again to get my Montessori certification. They were there. They even danced at my wedding.

I also learned from the stories of the group. Meeting after meeting, story after story, we discovered similarities between our experiences. We had been medicated for anxiety or depression. We had doubted our choices of careers. We had come to teaching in a less than linear way. We had been frustrated by the endless reflecting on our reflections we were asked to do in teacher training. We were frustrated by the types and quality of the feedback we were receiving from our supervisors, cooperating teachers, and mentors. We were reassured by the common threads we shared.

Our early meetings were simply an outlet, a place to be honest. In a very short amount of time, we had created a family. We knew such strange things about each other compared to what you'd know about a friend because we shared things you wouldn't typically share with relatively new friends, especially regarding mental health. Our group worked because everybody felt safe. Sometimes it wasn't okay to be emotional at work (especially as a woman). Tears were seen as a sign of weakness or unprofessionalism. At our meetings, we took our turns crying and no one thought we shouldn't be doing that. Tears were recognized a healthy outlet, a release for our repressed frustrations. What truly emerged for me at that table, surrounded by powerful, thoughtful women was the realization that language—narration and storytelling—is powerful in helping me construct my identity as teacher.

Writer's Workshop: Work of the Hand

Anna emailed the group asking us to bring artifacts to examine over our three-day summer workshop. Our first object was supposed to represent a struggle, and somewhat ironically, I struggled to decide what to bring. That summer I was entering my second year of graduate school for my Montessori training, and I was overwhelmed, trying to juggle all of my obligations. I knew I wanted to represent the struggle of time, but what concrete item would do that? I settled on a piece of embroidery my grandma had done, and I wrote a dialogue between myself and the object.

Figure 3: Grandma's Embroidery
Source: Author

Embroidery: Why work? Why go to school?

Me: To make money. To better my career. To make a difference in children's lives. Because the world tells me I should want to. That I am less of a person if I am not earning a living, especially since I don't have kids to mask the fact that I really just want to stay home and make beautiful things.

I laughed at the shock of my group members when I shared my writing. "You want to stay home and make things? Why is this the first time we're hearing about this?" I had never talked about teaching myself to knit in high school, followed by teaching myself to crochet in college. They didn't know that I'd been using hand work as a form of stress release for years or that my mom used to send me care packages loaded with coloring books and new boxes of crayons while I was in college. They didn't know the fulfillment I found in finishing a flawless sweater. The joy in following a pattern, catching mistakes, and fixing them. I was admitting to the group for the first time that I had aspirations outside of teaching and that the lack of a pattern to follow in the classroom made me question my desire to teach.

I have a strong perfectionist streak, which means a lot of my choices are influenced by my desire to live up to my perceptions of things I should be: I should be married by the time I'm twenty six. I should have children by the time I'm twenty-eight. I should have a job that offers a steady paycheck (teaching) instead of one that speaks to my creative side (theater). I should balance my career, my family, and my friends without fatigue. I should never let anyone down.

SHOW TIME

I fell into my first teaching job in a serendipitous way. I walked into the diverse, urban Montessori brick building anticipating an interview for an afterschool program position and walked out with a long-term substitute job in a fourth- and fifth-grade classroom, starting the following week.

I was given a tour and introduced to my new team. I noticed all of the comforting marks of a school: scuffed floors, kid-sized tables and chairs, the smell of books and pencil shavings. It felt like home, except there were very few exterior windows in the classrooms. Apparently, the architects felt exterior windows would jeopardize the safety of the students. The natural light flooded the hallways and only passed into classrooms through frosted windows at ceiling height and small windows in the classroom doors. I noticed an abundance of plants in the classrooms, and I wondered about their lack of sun. I asked one of my new team members how the plants survived in the dark. "We move them to the hallway on Fridays so they can soak up sun over the weekend," she responded.

I met my new team members. They seemed excited to meet me and share their insights about what my students would be like and how my classroom had been run. I was walking into a classroom in February after two previous teachers had already left. They offered advice, materials, and supplemental staff support. I noticed their eagerness in welcoming someone new to their team. I felt their passion, yet as my job got underway, I felt they were tired too. I noticed a feeling of division between experienced and novice teachers, a divide between traditional and progressive philosophies.

When I arrived for my first day, the classroom was in complete chaos. Under the previous teacher, very little instruction had been delivered. She would often go to the other teachers and exclaim, "They were so horrible! I didn't teach anything today!" I sensed fear when I walked in. I watched how the students looked at each other with sideways glances. I noticed how they carefully protected their personal belongings. I saw that there were two students in particular who others seemed to steer clear of and differ to in moments of conflict.

When I was hired, the principal told me, "Your job is to keep them safe." I wasn't sure how to accomplish safety in the tense classroom, but I knew how to play school, so I put on my teacher role. I followed the pattern of what I had learned in teacher training and tried to make something beautiful. We had daily classroom meetings, presented "All About Me" bags, set social and academic goals for the rest of year, and earned individual and group rewards.

My principal had told me to give it a month before I assessed how things were going. "A month," she said. "You'll see. It will take a month to feel like you're making progress." I put my whole self into the act of that month. I crossed off the days on a calendar by my desk. There was my progress. I could see it even if I didn't feel it. Slowly, my community-building games were met with fewer eye rolls. Slowly, personal belongings were not so heavily guarded. Two weeks in, a student left a note of my desk: "Thank you for being such a great teacher and fixing our class."

As the marks on the calendar got closer to a full month, most of the students were on board with the new normal. I was more confident in my performance as teacher. I was more comfortable dealing with the unknown and adjusting my plans mid-show. But there was one student whose trust I had not earned. He was distrusting of not only me, but also of anyone white. No matter how I addressed him, I was racist.

"Time to line up for lunch. Join us, please."

"You're racist."

"You need a pencil for lesson."

"You're racist."

"Take a break until you're ready to participate."

"You're racist."

"I noticed you remembered your book for silent reading."

"You're racist."

I realized that he must have a gotten a strong reaction out of others by using the word "racist." Of course, he was probably also reacting to the systemic racism of school and had found some inkling of power in the word "racist." It feels strange to mention systemic racism in a sentence because I know it is so much more than a sentence-long issue, much more than I understand. I am not an expert on this, but I know that racism lurks in schools, and in our interactions there.

It occurs to me now that he might have been reacting to me as representative of a system that has historically and currently undervalued the black body. So, as the rest of the class was coming around, I focused on finding ways to gain his trust, too. I "caught" him following expectations. I asked him about what he did outside of school. We agreed that taking a break in my classroom wouldn't mean a phone call home but going to take a break in another classroom would. One day I handed him a positive note to take home to his mom. Another student was refusing to do something I had asked, and he, raising his note home high in the air, said, "No, dude. You should do it. She's totally got your back if you do."

Breaking Character

Despite my sense of triumph, I was emotionally exhausted. I knew how to play teacher so I received a lot of praise for my work, but I still worried if I was doing enough. We had only been together as a class since February, but by the time we made it to spring break, I was so fatigued from meeting my students' needs and trying to live up to what I perceived to be my colleagues' expectations that I started crying every night after school. Some days, I didn't even make it home before the tears arrived. I would shut my door, sit at my desk, and cry. Every first-year teacher I know has stories about the crying they've done: I'm guessing you've cried too, or you will soon. My crying was real, and the fact that we cry about our students is real, too. I cried for the mountain of work I faced. I cried for the boy who was still reading at a first-grade level after months of intervention. I cried for the girl who really just wanted to sit in the corner and read all day. I cried for the girl who still hadn't mastered subtraction with regrouping and for the one who wanted to do an independent algebra project. I cried for the boy who wanted to make friends and couldn't understand why no one wanted to play with him after he spent the day stealing pencils and knocking notebooks to the floor. I cried for feeling my put-together teacher act slipping through my fingers as I desperately tried to hold on. I cried for not being enough.

I mostly cried because I thought I knew what teaching was. I thought I could follow the pattern I had learned watching my mom. I thought I would be able to see my mistakes and fix them. But a classroom of children does not make for a flawless sweater. The mistakes I made couldn't be fixed by removing a few stitches and starting over. I cried because I did not have control.

After observing me at the end of the school year, the principal said, "I just can't believe you're a first-year teacher," and offered me a job for the following school year if I was willing to attend Montessori training. I accepted, hoping that starting the next school year with a fresh start in my own classroom would mean an easier year. Because Montessori means multi-age classrooms, my class would be half returning students and half new. Surely, that meant that my hard work from the previous year would carry over. And in some ways, it did. They knew my routines and were able to help support the new students in learning the classroom. Starting the year with the students meant I had a little stronger plan, a little clearer picture of where I was going, but I was still emotionally exhausted at the end of every day. I wasn't at home anymore.

Set Change

In the spring of the next school year, an instructor from my Montessori training called.

"How do you like your current school?" he said.

I hesitated before answering. "I like it. It's good."

"Well, we're going to having an opening here next year. Would you be interested?"

"Maybe? Can I think about it and call you back?"

"Yes, but let me know soon. I want you on our team."

I was excited that my professor had thought of me, but I didn't know a lot about his school. He told stories in my graduate school classes about the work he did with his students, and I perceived a higher level of academic content than I was used to teaching, a more even distribution of student achievement. I knew the school was in a more affluent neighborhood in the city, had heard my current teammates make a few offhanded remarks about the luxury those teachers enjoyed, but I had never been there.

As soon as I hung up the phone, I called a peer from Montessori training to ask her opinion. I knew she had visited his school to observe there, so I wanted to know what she had seen.

"There's an opening at our professor's school next year. He wants me to have it."

"You have to say yes! That school is beautiful. The students are so focused. They are really independent. There are walls of windows in every room. The day I was there, there were five volunteers in helping! I would teach there if I could."

Her description was tempting. A wall of windows in every room! After spending a year and a half in a concrete box, I was giddy to imagine a classroom with more than fluorescent lights, and I wouldn't have to move my plants to the hallway every Friday. I was excited to imagine a classroom full of focused, independent students. It sounded a lot easier than what I was currently doing.

The next day, I went for a run with Amanda and told her about the offer and my perceptions of the school. She said, "You get to teach, not manage and battle and cry." I called my professor back and told him I was interested.

ASSUMPTIONS AND TRUTHS

The air between my colleagues and I became a little more tense, a little heavier, a little more hostile after I told them I was leaving. Some of these things were said to my face. Others were said to team members when I wasn't around. I felt them in the sideways glances and whispered conversations on my last day at the school. They made so many assumptions:

"She's leaving because she doesn't want to work with black kids."

"She doesn't like us."

"She hates the principal."

"She had one of the most difficult students in upper elementary. She's leaving because of him."

"She snuck around behind everyone's backs to find a new job."

"She should have told us earlier."

These assumptions bothered me more than I wish they did, and they hurt.

I *was* looking for a different path. I struggled with the truth that by seeking a classroom where I could perform my practiced role as teacher, I was choosing a whiter classroom. I struggled with the truth that the culture of school is, historically and currently, white. By choosing a different path, I was giving up the ability to learn about diverse cultures through the eyes of my students who embodied them. By choosing a different path, I was seeking a place where the pattern might be a little more straightforward, where the progress might be more obviously seen.

I was especially uneasy because I assumed I would be perceived as less of a teacher for going to a richer, whiter school. I knew that teachers in rich, white schools appeared to have it easy, and that some of the assumptions my colleagues made were firmly rooted in that idea. Upon hearing about my new job, one teacher at my first school told me, "You know that they don't use the fluorescent lights in their rooms because their PTA paid for floor and table lamps and the cord covers to make them safe? We can't get enough notebooks and they're getting floor coverings?" When I visited my new school, I had watched the children come calmly to their classroom meetings, sit criss-cross applesauce on the floor, and walk in silent, straight lines down the hallways because they knew how to play "student." Unfortunately, I knew my choice was a racially loaded one because the students walking silently down the hall were overwhelmingly white.

Being a self-taught knitter, it took me a long time to learn the technique of carrying a length of yarn behind a work in order to make two color patterns. If you've ever looked at the inside of knit hat or sweater made from more than one color, you've probably seen neat straight lines where the invisible color is carried along until it is used in the visible pattern again. My first attempts to master this technique did not yield beautiful, neat, straight lines. The front of my fabric was near perfect, with the colors showing up in the right places, but the back of the work was a loopy, tangled mess. It took me several projects to determine how to pick up the carried yarn every few to stitches so the loops were a little more contained, to get the tension right so all the stitches appeared the same from the front, to feel that I had found a way to balance the seen and unseen. Teaching was a lot like my first carried-yarn projects: Outwardly, I presented a near-perfect embodiment of teacher: on time, professionally dressed, prepared, savvy to the performance of school. But hidden on the other side was the tangled, loopy mess of my desire to balance work and school, to unravel my understanding of how to be the best teacher for my students of color when I knew they would learn best from teachers who looked like them, to reject the ideal teacher image I felt like I should live up to. The role that I had so carefully crafted was being undermined by my increasingly discontented understanding of the stereotypes my own classroom perpetuated. And I was so tired from trying to keep up the act. I felt like a character that had fallen into the wrong play.

Even so, I wrestled with the decision of whether or not to leave.

"They gave me my first job."

"I owe them so I should stay."

"They supported me when students were difficult."

"I owe them so I should stay."

"I bring fresh ideas to the team."

"I owe them so I should stay."

And then I realized, how did I end up in so much debt? I was the team member with the least amount of experience, and I felt that I needed to prove myself. I perceived a culture among my colleagues that said, "I can give you this, but only if you have something for me." I felt my performance as teacher was only as successful as the amount of valuable material I could offer. I was scrambling to come up with enough ideas to stay out of debt, all the while scrambling to stay caught up with all my other job requirements, my students' social-emotional needs, my graduate-school work, and my own well-being.

I am a fixer, and I could see the list of needs to meet as a growing, increasingly insurmountable task. But I knew how to play teacher, and I had practiced my role day after day. It should have been getting easier. I should have been able to meet every need, every day. I should have felt that "I'm a teacher now" moment. As the moment didn't come and the needs grew, so did my panic and guilt. I couldn't possibly be everything I supposed to be. There weren't enough hours in the day.

I felt guilty and ashamed of my inability to live up my perceptions of the ideal teacher. And worse, in leaving, I felt guilty that my students would finish their upper-elementary experience with a different teacher. As much as not being enough weighed on me, I loved those kids. I wanted to be everything for them.

Sometimes when I think back on all we accomplished in my first classroom, I wonder if I made the right choice in leaving. I convince myself that I could have stayed a little longer, just until Ayuub made it to a second grade reading level or until Asha could subtract with regrouping. I could have stayed to make sure Mahad got the behavior support he needed, and Ava found the confidence to speak above a whisper. And then I remember crying at my desk every day. Distance allowed me to see the pretty fabric we had created and helped me forget about the tangled mess behind it, but when I was living with the work, the loopy mess had me inexorably entangled. I lost sight of the successes because they were hidden in my attempt to perfect the role of teacher.

There was the scary reality that the assumptions other people made about me might be true. Perhaps my strong, defensive reaction to their assumptions meant that I should be changing something about my teaching practice, or even scarier, something that was fundamentally part of me. I once had a mentor teacher who said it took her a year after attending Beyond Diversity training to realize how systemic racism is and how many things she was doing to perpetuate cultural norms. I am afraid that after all of my reflections, I might wake up one day and realize that I was wrong about the truth of my motivation to leave my job, that other people's judgments of me were right.

Yet, I still walked into my new school and basked in the glory of a wall full of windows. I was energized by the daily dose of vitamin D. I picked out my first-day-of-school outfit, prepared my plan, brushed up on my teacher character. I was sure that this was the year I would say, "I'm a teacher now."

I took the job hoping that I wouldn't burn out, that I could teach in a way that fulfilled me. I took the job hoping that rather than merely surviving the day-to-day, I might have enough time to figure out how to make my performance as teacher feel more natural and fit better with the space in which I was teaching.

CONCLUSION

I have discovered part of my truth: my first job was unsustainable for me. There were too many children with too many needs, and my heart broke every time I realized all the ways I would fail to meet their needs. My compassion for each and every one of them weighed too heavily on me to sustain the job. I felt stuck.

There were so many parts of my job that I felt like there was nothing I could do to feel better. I could care about my students and teach them, but I felt I could never change the world they'd walk out into. My perfectionism meant I wasn't okay with knowing I was doing the best I could with the factors I could control. Like a dropped stitch that goes undiscovered until several rows later, I was too stuck on things I couldn't fix.

I wish I could say that I didn't judge other teachers, that I was exempt from the assumptions I faced in leaving. That I stood up to the harsh judgments of others without joining in. But I watched in disgust as a colleague walked out the door at 3:00 (the official end of our duty day) with nothing but her purse. Who did she think she was? She couldn't possibly be getting enough done if she wasn't taking work home. She wasn't playing teacher.

The act of playing teacher is rooted in my identity in and out of the classroom, and yet my experience has slowly unraveled my ability to play the part so easily. I am beginning to understand how playing teacher means perpetuating a broken system that only creates spaces for children willing and able to play student. The longer I am part of this performance, the clearer it is that we need a new script.

CHAPTER SIX

Profound Thoughts on a Bathroom Wall

BY SAMANTHA SCOTT

I am Sam.
Crazy cat lady, loves hip hop
My students don't steal my pens
Leaving again, still trying to smile

Don't cry, they can't handle it
Keep crying, hopefully they feel bad

I like reflecting on my reflections
Because it reminds me how I felt
While going through my grad program
Learning to teach, teaching for real

Went to Georgia, shared in Athens
We are writing a fucking book

What do we do here?

On September 24, 2013, Audrey gave us a writing prompt: What do we do here? I wrote: "We talk, share, laugh, cry. We offer support, give advice, and share funny stories. We are a strong intelligent group of women who aspire to be educators."

Before graduate school ended, before student teaching, before having my own classroom, I was meeting with a group of women. They were my teachers, my classmates, my colleagues, my friends, but ultimately they were my creative cohort, that gathered monthly as a form of survival. They were part of my self-care plan. They provided support, they let me cry and work through my demons. They reminded me why I decided to become a teacher. Together, we created a space outside of our graduate-school classrooms and eventually outside of our own classroom to learn and grow, and to be brave.

I was intentional about the group. I had never been involved in extra-curricular activities so I wanted my contribution to this group to be important and meaningful. I bought new pens and a green Moleskine notebook from Target. I placed a cat sticker I had purchased from the Internet Cat Video Festival that previous summer right in the middle of my new notebook to mark it as mine. This green Moleskine notebook with the cat sticker was now a place to hold my deepest darkest secrets about teaching.

Every month, I brought my notebook and a handful of my favorite pens and sat at Audrey's table with the intention of pouring my heart out to a group of women who truly understood the pain, agony, and triumphs that becoming (and being) a teacher brought. Some days, I didn't want to share. Instead, I would listen with my head down as I drew intricate doodles in my green moleskin notebook. It calmed me. It kept my mind from wandering. It allowed me to stay focused and be present while the others were talking. Audrey later pointed out that this was how I spent the first half of her methods class, head down, doodling, which isn't surprising since that was how I spent a good portion of graduate school, staff meetings, or trainings. Even the first time I met Anna.

Each month it seemed like we uncovered parts of ourselves that we rarely shared with others. A few months into our meetings, we learned that everyone around the table had battled, or was currently battling, demons in many forms. My personal experience with battling my own demons started in high school and has followed me through the last decade. It was comforting knowing that I wasn't alone.

I Wanted More for Us

Eventually, I reached a point where sitting around Audrey's table talking about how hard it was being a teacher wasn't enough. These women had so much passion and fire inside of them. I wanted more for us. I wanted us to channel our passion and fire into something with meaning outside of the safety and comfort of Audrey's table. And then we met Anna.

During our first meeting with Anna, I mostly kept my head down, doodling, while listening to her tell her story. She shared that she had taught overseas and had moved back to the States with her husband to start graduate school at the University of Minnesota. She shared that she had battled with her mental health her whole life. While I was doodling (and listening!), Anna shared her fear of what others would think of her if she disclosed she was bipolar in a school setting. I wrote down something she said in my green notebook that stood out to me: "Anna has a new idea, she must be manic. Anna is not doing anything, she must be depressed."

I knew *those* two feelings very well. The simplified way Anna explained her concerns about what others would think of her diagnosis was important to me because that was what I thought of myself. I flip-flopped between them, but spent a majority of my time in depressive episodes. Either I wasn't doing anything and sleeping all the time because I was depressed or I wasn't sleeping and had tons of great ideas.

Wild Horses/Writer's Workshop

In June 2015, we had our first writer's workshop. Anna asked us to bring an artifact that represented a struggle. I brought my empty Adderall container. I chose it because my psychiatrist had adjusted my medication (meds) the month prior. To make an adjustment to my meds was a process. To even accept that I needed meds in the first place was a process. To accept that the medication I had been taking was no longer working the way it should have was a process. When that happened, it made me feel that I wasn't "getting better." It was a reminder that all of this was an ongoing struggle. It made me feel like it was taking me further away from my ultimate goal: I did not want to need medication to manage my mental health. I continued to fight this internal battle.

Artifacts

Anna asked us to engage with our artifact:

> Who are you?
> I am Sam's empty Adderall bottle.
> Why are you here?
> Sam thought I represented a struggle.
> What do you do?

I am prescribed to people who have narcolepsy and attention deficit disorders.... Sam couldn't finish this activity because she started googling information about me and got distracted.

Then she had us trade our artifacts with another teacher and asked them to write from the perspective of that artifact. I traded with Anna and she wrote about the bottle: "I have a special top. It screws on tight keeping the inside safe. My directions are printed neatly on the label for you to read and follow. Don't change things up on your own, it is my job to keep you stable. What is missing is how you might feel when you miss a dose or take too many. Maybe I am not even the right one for you. But if I am, you can refill me over and over until you can't live without me."

Every time I read the lines: "It is my job to keep you stable. You can refill me over and over until you can't live without me," I wanted to cry. The empty bottle represented my instability. And it was true, I couldn't live without my meds because when I missed a dose, I was light-headed and sick to my stomach by the end of the day. If I missed a dose multiple days in a row my mood was no longer stable—I had a harder time controlling my emotions—making it impossible for me to live without my meds. This was the harsh reality I continue to struggle with to this day. I can't function without my medication.

Exploring artifacts like the Adderall bottle with Anna and the rest of my Wild Horses was an exercise in (re)narrating our stories. My empty Adderall bottle began to (re)narrate my struggle with my mental health. It was a tactile object that felt bare and empty in my hands, but represented the demons I have been trying to fight for the last decade of my life.

In a letter to Anna at the beginning of the writer's workshop sharing my goals for the summer writing project, I wrote: "I want to give myself a creative outlet to express myself and share a story, maybe mine, maybe someone else's.... I want to make sense of myself, my work, and my mental health. I want others to see what I see—with a crude/funny tone. I want to show people how I find the funny amidst the chaos."

The funny I was finding amidst the chaos was the graffiti students were leaving around the schools. The graffiti became the artifacts that would help me make sense of myself, my work, and my mental health.

Profound Thoughts: The Beginning

Figure 1:
Title: Honest Advertising
Artist: A clever young lady
Medium: Red Sharpie on metal
2014

What they say about teaching is true: you don't have time to go to the bathroom. When I started teaching, I stopped caring which restroom I used at school. The *luxurious* staff bathroom was on the other side of the building, but a student bathroom was within spitting distance of my classroom. Unfortunately, during the walk down the hall to the staff restroom, many things could happen: Someone could stop me to tell me about what one of my students was doing earlier, I could get distracted, I might need to stop by the office and talk to Ann, one of my students might come running around the corner, I might get to the bathroom and forget what I was even doing in the first place.

I thought the transition from the staff bathroom to the student bathroom would be harder than it was. I thought I would retreat back to the magical space where students weren't allowed. Then I saw it one day after school in the girl's bathroom. The picture that may have saved me.

There it was, written in red Sharpie on the feminine hygiene dispenser: woman diapers and vigina stuffers. I was beside myself. This was the best thing I had seen all day, no wait, all year. I whipped out my iPhone and quickly snapped a picture because I HAD TO SHOW EVERYONE RIGHT NOW. (See how easily I get distracted? I wasn't lying.) Surely everyone would find this as funny as I did. Who was I going to show first?! Ann. Ann was the first one I needed to show. She would love it. Since Ann was at the other end of the building, she ended up not being the first person I showed because I ran into five other teachers on my way to the office who I knew would enjoy the picture as much as me. I watched my colleagues as they squinted at my screen, their faces turned from concentration to disbelief to amusement. It was hilarious to see "woman diapers" and a misspelled "vigina" on a feminine hygiene machine. We could teach new spelling lists every week and have students practice daily, but someday, somewhere, they were going to take a red Sharpie, take what they've learned, and use it in real life. It was the most brilliant thing I had seen all year.

After spending forty-five minutes of my precious student-free-work-time I made it back to my classroom. I felt lighter. In those brief moments of shared laugher, I was reminded of why I was here. Amidst the chaos of teaching, I found humor on our very own school walls, waiting to be seen. I decided this was too good to keep to myself. Everyone needed to see it. I took the liberty of posting it on Instagram and Facebook and sharing it with the rest of my friends and family. I added a title and artist and listed the medium and date for good measure. Because in my eyes, it was a work of art that needed to be appreciated from all perspectives. It didn't take long for people to start liking and commenting. The first comment came from a colleague, "A spelling lesson was needed, but the honesty and clear language of the graffiti is appreciated."

I started to pay attention to the graffiti I was finding around school. Finding graffiti became my way of coping with being a teacher. These pictures were shedding some light on what it was like being a teacher. The art was telling my stories of what it was like to be a teacher. More importantly, the art was telling stories of my students.

Once I started posting the graffiti art, it didn't take long for my teacher friends to share art they found too. But I needed more people to find graffiti in the schools, so I enlisted two young souls (thanks G and L!) to scope out the art at their schools. And, soon there was no shortage of penis drawings and swear words. I noticed how the graffiti that came from the high school started getting more complex and dark than what I found in my K-8 building. The youth were communicating through their graffiti art. I began to wonder who the artists were trying to communicate with.

Profound Thoughts: Fuch vs. Fuck

Figure 2:
Title: Fuch vs. Fuck
Artist(s): Unknown
Medium: Pencil on white walls
2014

It was like the art found me. Every corner I turned, there was another masterpiece to be discovered. Some days, I didn't even have to look. Other teachers would alert me to the new art that was popping up around the school. When I first heard about this piece of art, it was just "fuch." But by the time someone took a picture and passed it to me, another young artist had added a line, turning "fuch" into the word we all know and some love, "fuck." That night I posted it on Facebook, which lead to a hilarious thread between my colleagues who had seen the art in person.

"At least they spelled it correctly! Yeah for teaching the 'ck' sound!" (CD)
"JB's kids found it and I just had to capture it for the art expert! (ER)
"I think I erased that! Or a similar sentiment on the wall opposite J's classroom. Some second graders pointed it out and said 'but it's missing Y-O-U!'" (RP)
"I read the rough draft before the spelling error was addressed. It is getting there. Maybe tomorrow it won't just be a sentence fragment." (CB)

These pictures were building community. They were creating dialogue between my teacher friends. They were opening up important conversations about teaching and students for my Facebook friends who didn't work in education. These pictures were telling our stories as teachers.

Profound Thoughts: Pop Culture Musings

Figure 3:
Title: Deez Nuts
Artist: Unknown
Medium: Green Sharpie on tile
2015

If you're a teacher or spend any time with kids, you've most likely seen or heard the phrase "deez nuts." If you're unfamiliar with "deez nuts," it started as a six-second video on the popular social media app Vine. The phrase "deez nuts" has been appropriated by youth and some adults, and according to Urban Dictionary it can be used as a response (to nearly everything) to annoy others. For example, a special-ed math teacher might ask, "What's the absolute value of -8?" And a charming seventh grade student may respond, "DEEZ NUTS!" It generally starts out funny if used in the right context, but when you're trying to teach a math lesson, or trying to have a serious conversation with middle schoolers, it is annoying AF (which stands for "as fuck," my new favorite abbreviation; thanks kids!).

As a teacher who has spent countless hours with students of all ages, I've had the honor of learning the latest slang and pop-culture references. Thanks to popular Vines, YouTube videos, and music, there is a never-ending list of words most teachers hear on any given day. Just when you think it's over and they've moved on to the next latest phrase, you might make the mistake of using the word *thought* in a sentence, and an eighth-grader might start giggling and say to the class, "She said THOT!" THOT is an unfortunate abbreviation for That Hoe Out There, which might be my least favorite slang word since it is generally used as a derogatory term towards girls.

Some may be offended. Some may believe the slang words that our students use don't belong in the classroom. I would argue that ignoring their acquired literacies doesn't serve us well. In fact, slang gives us access to what our students think and feel. I continue to be interested in the meaning of slang words and what their use might say about my students' literacies. While it's true that certain words could be right or wrong in the context of school, it's also true that those same words can give us a better understanding of our students.

Profound Thoughts: Teenage Angst

Figure 4:
Title: Teenage Angst
Artist: Angsty teenager
Medium: Black Sharpie on white walls
September 2014

There were pieces of carrots everywhere and it *had* to be him. No one else would chew up carrots and put them on Darren's desk and watch with a lifeless face as he exploded with anger.

Darren had a stack of books on his desk so he could move on to the next book without skipping a beat. Half-finished drawings, worksheets, and a variety of different-colored Sharpies and fine-point drawing pens filled the open spaces of his desk. Instead of melting into a pile on the floor when he became frustrated like he did in the past, he would hide behind his stack of books and take heavy breaths until he calmed down. He even had a chair he had claimed since the beginning of the year. If someone took it, he would track it down and quickly push it back to his desk, smirking. He owned that space. That chair was *his*. Those sharpies, drawings, and books? They were *his*. It's how he played school. He had made tremendous gains over the years, and as an eighth-grader, he finally felt successful at school. So when he came back to class, and found carrots that someone had chewed up and spit onto his desk, he lost his shit. And he couldn't hide behind his books, because then he would be lying on top of regurgitated carrots someone had left on *his* desk, on *his* drawings, in *his* space.

When Darren started to lose his shit, I started to put together what had happened, and I froze. *I* am supposed to know what to do when a student chews up carrots and spits them on another student's desk. *I* am supposed to know how be proactive instead of reactive. *I* am supposed to have created a classroom culture where students didn't chew up their snacks and spit them on their classmates' desks.

I watched them, terrified that Darren was going to punch Bobby square in the face. I watched them, wondering how Bobby was going to respond. I watched them, because I didn't know what else to do.

Should I jump over the desks like superwoman and get in-between them to block the inevitable blows? Should I scream and distract them? Instead, I did the only thing I could do—nothing. I stayed planted in my spot in the front of the class, while the rest of the students watched in excitement at what could possibly happen next. Darren was known to be explosive. Bobby was known to be vicious with his words. Anything was possible.

Darren stood over Bobby. Bobby looked up at him with a blank face. He remained unfazed by the fact that one of the most volatile students in the classroom was screaming at him because he had put chewed up carrots on his desk. I was thinking, "This is it, this is when Darren is going to punch him in the face. Bobby deserves it. Is it wrong for me to say that? I can't stop it! I'm in the front of the classroom. They are in the back of the classroom. It's going to happen. Oh shit oh shit oh shit. I should look away. I can't. I'm going to have to write this up. I need to be able to write every detail down. Fuck fuck fuck fuck what do I do?!?!?!"

My internal monologue stopped when Darren rushed to the door, shoving the large circular table into the wall on his way out. I let out a huge sigh of relief before I looked at Bobby, who was now waiting for me to react. He loved watching me. He had been watching me all year, analyzing how I reacted to different situations.

Without thinking, I started yelling at Bobby. I told him how awful he was. I told him how rude he was. I told him that there was no one else in the classroom I could sit him next to because they had all had enough of him. Warm tears started streaming down my face as I screamed at him to get out of my classroom. He looked at me dead in the eyes and said, "fucking bitch." My tears dripped down my face faster as he left the classroom and the rest of my students shuffled in from their second period class.

I didn't cry because he called me a fucking bitch. I cried because Bobby and the chewed-up carrots represented something bigger. They represented a larger systematic "brokenness" that I have experienced working with the special-education population. This child had been failed on so many levels and had no control over his life. He lived in chaos but was expected to go to school and follow the rules and expectations we had created for him. I cried because I yelled at someone who was trying to grasp onto what little control he had. I cried because I didn't know what else to do. I cried because I didn't have control. I cried because control is an illusion.

I cried because they don't teach you in teacher school what you're supposed to do when a kid who has no control over his life chews up carrots and spits them on to his classmate's desk.

Profound Thoughts: *Poop*

Figure 5:
Title: Poopy
Artist: Timid pooper
Medium: Pen on wall
2015

I was exhausted. I was over the edTPA. I was broke. I had a broken toe and a needy girlfriend and I wanted to be done. Done with school. Done with working for free. Done with all the fucking reflecting. I was about to have my last observation as a student teacher and I was determined to end it on a good note so that I could finish that chapter of my life and move on to the next one.

I was nervous about my final observation. I was teaching a math lesson on percentages to a group of obnoxious eighth-graders. It may have been the most immature grouping of kids possible and my cooperating teacher and I had been struggling with them since the beginning of the year. I was nervous that they were going to ruin my run of perfect evaluations. My lesson involved making estimates and finding fractions and percentages with M&Ms. I was hoping the candy would at least make the math less painful. It turned out to be a fun lesson. The students were mostly engaged, a little rowdy and giggly, but typical eighth-grade behavior.

I was about fifteen minutes into my lesson when the giggling wouldn't stop. I stood up from the document camera where I had been modeling how to record the data from our M&M activity. I took a few steps away from the desk (that's some Envoy shit right there) and I watched the students. They watched me as I watched them. I listened. It didn't take long until I figured out what was happening.

"Poop."

There it was, the four-letter word that never seemed to get old. I'll admit that I still find bathroom humor to be hilarious, but my student-teaching supervisor was behind me, so I immediately started sweating because she might not find bathroom humor as amusing as I did. She was also watching me and writing down everything that I was doing, including how I responded to my obnoxious students. "How do I respond to my students who no longer can do their math because they're laughing about poop?" I pleaded with myself. "What the fuck do I do? Please, don't start laughing, Sam. You're their teacher! Make them get it together!"

Fuck it. I decided to join them. "Poop." The students stopped laughing. They stared at me. They glanced at each other. A few of them covered their mouths and attempted to hold in their laughter. They looked back at me. I kept going, "You poop. I poop. We all poop." Then they completely lost it. Laughter would no longer be contained, and I had completely lost control of my class. Fuck. FUCK. FUUUCKKKKK.

Breathe, Sam.

BREATHE.

It's okay.

They're immature.

They're developmentally incapable of not losing their shit over shit.

Poop is hilarious.

I might even shit my pants right now. Shitting my pants would be hilarious.

In my head I started yelling. "SHUT UP! STOP IT! I AM BEING WATCHED! I'M NEVER GOING TO BE ABLE TO BE A TEACHER SINCE I CAN'T CONTROL A GROUP OF 8TH GRADERS!!!"

When I got into situations like this, I always imagined a big dramatic scene where I yelled and knocked everything over like they do in the movies. Instead, I stood there in silence with a blank look on my face and watched the scene unfold in front of me. Finally, I came back to reality. I remembered the time I once asked a veteran teacher how she did it every day. Her response was that you either laugh or cry. Since poop is funny, I laughed.

A few years later during our writer's workshop, I revisited the evaluation from the giggly poop lesson. I remember the post observation going over well with my advisor. She had a special education background and totally got it. She had laughed with me.

In reference to the whole poop fiasco, her evidence and comments section read, "They [students] were loud and enthusiastic. She [teacher] demonstrates a mature response to suggestions and promptly addresses areas that might need revision."

Profound Thoughts: *Demons*

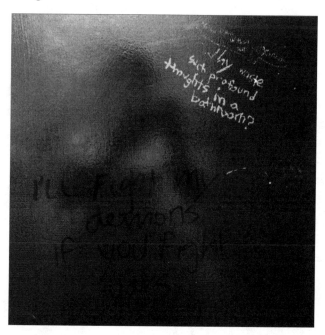

Figure 6:
Title: Profound Thoughts in the Bathroom
Artist(s): Teenage philosophers
Medium: Black Sharpie and scratched paint on bathroom stall
September 2015

After collecting student "artwork" over the course of my few years as a teacher, I started to wonder if the graffiti the students were leaving on the walls of (our) schools was something bigger, something louder, something more profound than just swear words and penises being scribbled on the bathroom walls.

The day I saw this particular work of art was when I really started looking at the writing on the walls differently. In the middle it said, "I'll fight my demons if you fight yours." Another student chimed in by scraping the paint of the bathroom stall and wrote, "Why waste such profound thoughts in a bathroom?" Profound thoughts in the bathrooms? THIS WAS PERFECT. I couldn't have come up with a better title myself. Up until this picture, it was all penises, swear words, and funny phrases. "Profound" implied that the artists had great knowledge and insight into what they were writing on the walls.

This wasn't silly, it wasn't foul, and it wasn't an act of rebellion. It was raw, honest, and real. Being a teenager is *hard*. As teachers, we can see the graffiti, roll our eyes, and be annoyed by the fact that the students are vandalizing *our* schools. Instead, I found myself asking: What are the students trying to tell us? What does it mean to them? Is the graffiti the students leave around the school their way of expressing themselves to us? Is this their way of marking their territory on the school walls, to remind us that this is their space too?

Profound Thoughts: *Last Words*

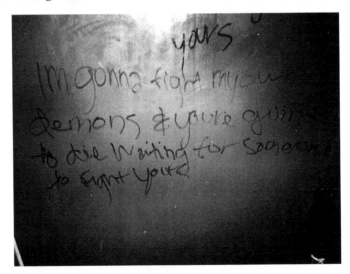

Figure 7:
Title: More Profound Thoughts in the Bathroom
Artist: Another teenage philosopher
Medium: Red Sharpie on the same bathroom stall
September 2015

I wanted to tell you about how sad I was in high school. I wanted to tell you about how I didn't fit in and no one understood me, but no matter what angle I used to spin it, it sounded like the typical mopey high school narrative. Not that my feelings at that time weren't valid, but it didn't sound much different from every other sad high schooler. What I can tell you is that the sadness never went away and at times, it became debilitating. I spent most of my teenage years and twenties in and out of depressive episodes attempting to fight my own personal demons. This led to poor grades, inconsistent school and work attendance, and strained relationships. I would try to explain to friends how sad I was and I would get blank looks in response. They told me to snap out of it. I wanted to tell them how hard I was trying, that I was using all of my energy to get out of bed. I would wake up hoping that today would be different. Instead, my body felt heavy and empty at the same time and I'd melt into my bed, terrified to face the world.

Do the students have anxiety on Sundays because they have to go to school the next day? Do they fall onto the couch when they get home after school because they're exhausted from trying to pretend they aren't hurting? Do they raid the fridge or alcohol cabinet to cope? Do they wake up dreading the day ahead of them?

It took me the last decade to truly understand my mental health and what I needed to fight my demons. In my teenage years and early twenties I didn't have the luxury of life experience to understand that it will get better and that I really am a unique tropical starfish (thanks Leslie Knope!). But those demons are real. Maybe you ignore them. Maybe you know they are there and you let them get comfortable, or maybe you have the strength to fight them. It took me a long time to find and build the strength to deal with my demons. My hope for the students with demons who reach out to us on the bathroom walls is that they will find the strength to fight their demons. I hope they win. I hope they learn to acknowledge their demons and fight them.

Every year, I seem to have an increase of students on my caseload who have significant mental-health needs. On top of teaching grade-level content, meeting PLC goals, and raising test scores, schools have to meet students' social and emotional needs. It can be an impossible job. I remember after a really painful middle-school meeting during my first year of teaching, a few of us lingered around trying to make sense of what was happening in our school. We had voiced our concerns to administration, some of us in tears, but they had no answers for us. We had our own ideas, thoughts, maybe even profound thoughts, but we didn't have a plan of action, because our job felt impossible. We asked ourselves, what do we do when we're not enough?

What I found on the bathroom walls were students with profound thoughts who wanted to be heard. We teachers may want to erase and cover up the things they say, but I think it's worth listening, for all of our sakes. We share the same space. School is a collective space for students and teachers. We need to support children and youth, teenagers and artists, as they travel through these spaces. Start listening.

Epilogue

BY THE WILD HORSES

We want to leave you with two images. The first is the woman, laptop in hand, who followed behind Aubrey in her classroom and recorded her every word and move. Rating, evaluating, and ultimately categorizing her as "not proficient." The second image is of all of us: at Audrey's table talking seriously; in Amanda's kitchen loading our plates with food; at Anna's cabin sharing our first writings as artifacts. Telling stories, feasting, and repositioning our struggles. As a collective, we know that we have effected change in our bodies and minds.

When we trust each other, we can interrupt each other. In our vulnerability and willingness to trust in the Wild Horses, we welcomed interruption and repositioning of our identities as teachers. We liked how that felt. This work cannot be done alone; it is in the story telling and story writing with others that we (re) narrate toward a sense of collective well-being.

~Audrey, Anna, Amanda, Aubrey, Marie, and Sam

sj Miller & Leslie David Burns
GENERAL EDITORS

Social Justice Across Contexts in Education addresses how teaching for social justice, broadly defined, mediates and disrupts systemic and structural inequities across early childhood, K–12 and postsecondary disciplinary, interdisciplinary and/or trans-disciplinary educational contexts. This series includes books exploring how theory informs sustainable pedagogies for social justice curriculum and instruction, and how research, methodology, and assessment can inform equitable and responsive teaching. The series constructs, advances, and supports socially just policies and practices for all individuals and groups across the spectrum of our society's education system.

Books in this series provide sustainable models for generating theories, research, practices, and tools for social justice across contexts as a means to leverage the psychological, emotional, and cognitive growth for learners and professionals. They position social justice as a fundamental aspect of schooling, and prepare readers to advocate for and prevent social justice from becoming marginalized by reform movements in favor of the corporatization and de-professionalization of education. The over-arching aim is to establish a true field of social justice education that offers theory, knowledge, and resources for those who seek to help all learners succeed. It speaks for, about, and to classroom teachers, administrators, teacher educators, education researchers, students, and other key constituents who are committed to transforming the landscape of schools and communities.

Send proposals and manuscripts to the general editors at:

sj Miller   sj.Miller@colorado.edu
Leslie David Burns   L.Burns@uky.edu

To order other books in this series, please contact our Customer Service Department at:

(800) 770-LANG (within the U.S.)
(212) 647-7706 (outside the U.S.)
(212) 647-7707 FAX

or browse online by series at:

WWW.PETERLANG.COM